CO-PILOTING

Co-Piloting
Luck, Leadership, and Learning That It's All About Others
Our Story

Published by Forefront Books in association with the
literary agency of Wolgemuth & Associates.

Cover Design by Bruce Gore, Gore Studio Inc.
Interior Design by Bill Kersey, KerseyGraphics

ISBN: 978-1-948-67758-5
ISBN: 978-1-948-67759-2 (eBook)
ISBN: 978-1-948-67738-7 (Audio)

CO-PILOTING

LUCK, LEADERSHIP, AND LEARNING THAT IT'S ALL ABOUT OTHERS

OUR STORY

JIM HASLAM

WITH JOHN DRIVER

Forefront
BOOKS

Dedicated to the Senior Leadership Team of
Pilot Company and our 28,000 team members
who serve others with excellence every day.

In memory of Team Members Denise Nibbe, Nettie Spencer, Joyce Whaley of the Stawberry Plains Travel Center: you will never be forgotten.

CONTENTS

SECTION I
THE BREAKS

SECTION 2

REFLECTIONS

FOREWORD

By Bill Haslam

I AM A LITTLE BIASED, BUT I THINK THE STORY BEFORE YOU IS UNIQUE, inspirational, and often hilarious. You should also know that it has been written against the will of its author. You don't see that every day, I know.

But then again, you don't meet many people like my dad every day.

As you will soon learn, Jim Haslam hates to *talk* about himself, so there was no way he was going to *write* about himself. His interests lie in many other places. His beloved wife, Natalie. His family. His faith. His community. His church. His alma mater. His endeavors in politics and philanthropy. And last, but certainly not least, the company he founded and the tens of thousands of employees (or team members, as Dad insists they always be called) who look up to him not only as a boss but, also as a role model—and even as a father figure.

But write about himself? That has never been in his playbook.

Despite all this, his family has been pestering him for years to write his story—and the story of Pilot Company, of course. As you will see, not only is his life story a great one, but he also has many great stories about his life. Our family has heard most of these stories many times around our family table—and we are excited that Dad has finally relented so that you might enjoy them as well.

Before he tells his side of the whole unlikely narrative, let me share a few thoughts as his youngest child—that is, one of the people, amid his many protests, who helped set into motion this whole process of putting his life story into a book.

There is a certain story that comes to mind that epitomizes what it was like to have Jim Haslam as a father. When he started Pilot, most of his gas stations were in southwest Virginia, so Dad constantly had to be there. It had taken every penny he owned or could borrow to build those first stations, and there was certainly no guarantee the company would make it. This meant he was away from home a lot. Yet somehow in my memory, Dad was always home. I still don't know how he was able to pull this off with his schedule, but the bottom line is that, whenever it mattered, Dad was always there.

I remember being seven years old and preparing to play my first Pee Wee baseball game. For whatever reason, it was really important to me that I have my own baseball cleats, not my brother's hand-me-downs. The day before the game, I told Dad that I really needed new cleats. To my dismay, he said he had to leave first thing the next morning for Virginia, so Mom would have to get them for me. That wasn't going to work. "Moms don't know how to buy baseball cleats!" In my seven-year-old brain, this felt like the end of the world.

The next day, I was at the ball field before the game, wearing my brother's hand-me-downs, of course. The baseball field was at the bottom of a hill. To this day, one of my most vivid memories is of my dad running full speed down that hill with a shoebox in his hands. I'm sure he blew off some important meeting to make it back in time, and I'm still not sure where he found the time to stop and buy baseball cleats. As a busy executive and father of three, he could've just said, "You're seven. It's a Pee Wee baseball game. You will be fine."

But he figured out a way to show up. And he still does. His children, step-children, grandchildren, and great-grandchildren can all tell you their own stories about how he has shown up and loved them well.

You will discover throughout the story to come that, despite his protests and constantly pushing away the limelight, my dad has accomplished so much in business, the community, and in politics. However, I honestly believe that he never did any of these things for himself. In fact, to understand who Jim Haslam really is as a person, you must understand that everything he has ever done has been done for other people: his family, the university he loves, and the community he feels has given him so much. Over the years, I have had hundreds of people I don't know stop me to tell of something my dad did for them in secret.

In his world, he is never just *giving*; rather, he is always *giving back*.

I have always been a little befuddled when people act as if my dad's efforts in community and political arenas are just "Big Jim" trying to use his power to pull strings and get his way. Anyone who actually knows him knows that this is not what he is about. He is an offensive lineman blocking for others to score touchdowns. His natural inclination is to be a team player, sometimes even to a fault.

Dad has always found time to invest in relationships, including being there for the people in these relationships. To be honest with you, I can't figure out how he has always found a way to help others so much. I have been in business and have spent time in public office, so I know that time is a difficult commodity to manage, much less manage *well*. However, it always seemed that Dad found a way to manage it better than anyone else, always being there to spend time with us. He was always coaching our Little League or sports teams. He was there for talks and trips to the beach.

The other kids in the neighborhood always wanted to play at our house so Dad could be the quarterback or pitcher for our backyard games. I now know how much he was doing in the community, how hard it is to build a business, and how he also somehow maintained a host of really close friendships through it all. Looking back—especially during his thirties and forties—I still can't figure out how he pulled it all together. Again, in my memory, he was simply always there.

There aren't enough words, but suffice it to say that having a father who is so loving, hardworking, full of integrity, fun, and optimistic has shaped my entire life. As Dan Fogelberg sang, "My life has been a poor attempt to imitate the man, I'm just a living legacy, to the leader of the band."

Sometimes I will be walking down the street and think of something funny that he either did or said, and I will smile all by myself. Well, as you read his story, you'll discover the heart of a remarkable man who is deeply loved and is the reason so many people are smiling. As you turn the page, now it's your turn to smile.

And Dad, enjoy the book...even if you really didn't want to write it.

CHAPTER I

UNEXPECTED INTRODUCTIONS

Burgers, Billionaires, and Big Questions

IT WAS PROBABLY JUST ANOTHER DAY TO MOST PEOPLE, BUT JULY 10, 2017, was one of the most interesting days of my life. At 10:00 a.m. that summer morning, I was riding up an elevator in a nice, but not overly impressive, office building in downtown Omaha. Joining me in the elevator were my older son, Jimmy Haslam, investment banker Byron Trott, and a security agent who was escorting our trio to our appointment on the top floor. When the elevator dinged its final ding and the doors opened, we were greeted by the smiling face and warm reception of the man we had traveled all the way from East Tennessee to meet.

He extended his hand and said, "Hi, I'm Warren Buffett."

Of course, we already knew who *he* was, so we introduced ourselves and the famed investor led us to his office. Now, if you know anything at all about Jimmy Haslam, you know my son tends to jump straight into matters of business; this day was no exception. But Warren interrupted him. "Hold on just a second." Turning to me, he asked, "Jim, how old are you?"

"I'm eighty-six years old."

"So am I!" he replied with a hint of growing interest, like a man putting a puzzle together piece-by-piece. "When is your birthday?"

"December 13, 1930."

"Really? Mine is August 30."

These days, most people can remember where they were on September 11, 2001. It is like a tragic right of passage in American culture for those old enough to own the memory. But Mr. Buffett had another question altogether. "Where were you on Pearl Harbor Day?" I couldn't help but laugh because there aren't many of us left in this world who have the sobering, yet high honor of answering that particular question.

Once we had gotten to know each other and had talked over some preliminary business matters for about an hour, Warren asked if we were hungry. We were, so we stepped back into the elevator and began heading down toward what I assumed would be a private dining room in the basement of the building, much like the ones we have at our Pilot Company[1] headquarters back in Knoxville. Instead, the elevator opened into a parking garage.

Warren asked me to ride with him in his car and suggested that Jimmy ride with Byron. As we rode along, we began a conversation about philanthropy, something we are both passionate about. I assumed we were going to a country club for lunch, but instead, after about a five-minute drive, we arrived at the Hilton hotel. We followed Warren through the front doors and into the lobby where he was greeted left and right by staff members of the hotel. He led us all the way to a corner table in the back section of a little lunch café. We took our seats just as a waitress arrived to take our orders.

"Hi, Susie!" Warren said with a smile.

---

1 The company name has had several variations over the years relative to what was happening during that time period. The names have included Pilot Oil Corporation, Pilot Flying J (PFJ), and Pilot Company. Throughout the pages to come I may use any of these names, but will most often refer to the company simply as Pilot.

"Hello, Mr. Buffett," she replied. "You want your usual, a cheeseburger and a Coke?"

This may have been *usual* for him, but this whole experience was very *unusual* for me. There we were, sitting at a corner table in a little café with the second-richest man in the world—and we were about to eat cheeseburgers! But just like most of the people I've crossed paths with over the years—from Army privates to company presidents, from small-town businessmen to big-city billionaires—I saw that Warren Buffet is just a regular guy. If anything, I'd say he's actually humbler than most.

> There we were, sitting at a corner table in a little café with the second-richest man in the world—and we were about to eat cheeseburgers!

It was one of those moments you never forget. In fact, in that moment, I found myself yet again asking the same question I've pondered many times over the course of this incredible life God has granted me: how in the world did this happen? That's the question I aim to address in this book.

And, though I usually don't drink them, I went ahead and ordered a Coke too. Hey, if it's good enough for Warren Buffett, I guess it's good enough for me!

I've Been Lucky

Mr. Buffet taught me more that day than how to enjoy an ice-cold Coca-Cola. Looking back, I know I took away many other unique and significant impressions from my time with him, just as I have done with so many other incredible people and experiences in my life. Each one has taught me something valuable. Even when the times have been rough, each one has made me a better man, even when it has taken some time to get there. Each one has contributed to my story in remarkable ways.

Though it is *my* name on the cover of this book and *my* story you're about to hear, it is really the stories of my interaction *with others* that I look forward to sharing the most. This is really *our* story, not mine. It is true that no man is an island; we are all connected, and these connections are what make any story—including mine—worth its salt.

This is the story of my family, our company, and me.

While my life has had its share of the same ups and downs that all people go through, I've had some unique experiences that my family feels just might leave you entertained, informed, and perhaps even encouraged or inspired. But if nothing else, I hope this is going to be *fun*.

We may not know each other, but as you've traveled down the interstate with your family, perhaps you've stopped for gas, coffee, or food at one of our Pilot Company locations and interacted with some of our 28,000 incredible team members. Regardless, you might be wondering why I am writing this book in the first place. There are three main reasons:

1. To tell this story for my family and friends.
2. To offer a personal history of Pilot Company from its beginnings in 1958 to the present.
3. To share principles and insights about what I think are really important in this world—things I have discovered (often the hard way) through living a full life beyond what I deserve.

Regarding the first reason, you need to know that I am writing this book under extreme duress—or, should I say, at the *loving insistence* of my wonderful family. For years, they have been not-so-gently prodding me to write my story. Penning my own autobiography and memoir was not something I set out to do, nor is it something I ever thought I *would* do. Certain friends—like the talented and hilarious Coach Rick Barnes, who, as you will read, actually had a dream about me writing this book— have long suggested that I do so, but I've never seriously considered it until now.

Writing your own story has plenty of positives and negatives. From a negative side, it may look like you think your story is important enough to be written, which seems self-serving. The truth is, I do not have even the slightest desire to attempt to wax eloquent about my successes and failures. This is not a book where you're going to watch me pat myself on the back. I don't deserve anything of the sort. Besides, self-back-patting doesn't make for very good reading, in my opinion. There are enough self-congratulating books out there, and I do not plan to add mine to the list.

But, as this story unfolds, there are some people I *do* want to pat on the back, and I think you will find they are more than worthy of accolades. The *people* in my story are the *positives* of my story—family, friends, mentors, Pilot Company team members—and how, together, we built the company. They are the reasons I have finally relented and agreed to write a book. The story is so tightly wound up in theirs that to tell mine is to tell theirs—and that is a prospect that makes me very happy.

I may not be a writer by trade, but I am a storyteller at heart, as any of my children, grandchildren, friends, or team members will attest. I love to reminisce about the details of the past, taking a stroll down Memory Lane just to see if the houses and lawns still look and smell the same as they did when I was there the first time. To that end, God has blessed me with what I think is a pretty decent memory for someone who is nearly ninety years old. Many of the stories you'll hear live in my memory as if they happened yesterday, and compiling them has been a worthwhile and fulfilling experience.

As I look back on these memories, I can't help but agree with my family and friends that I have indeed lived a blessed and eventful life. In fact, I beg you not to read these reflections only as the musings of a man who has been fortunate in business. Sure, I'll share insights about business, but that is only one side of our story. I have experienced faith, failure, hope, happiness, love, loss, and a host of other emotions and events—many of which will sound funny, even if only to hear how I got it wrong. But, if you really want to get down to brass tacks, mine is a story of *luck*, both in my personal life and in business. In fact, I recognize that much of what's happened to me does not happen to most people. In this respect, I have most definitely been lucky, something for which I am daily and eternally grateful.

However, I do think good things—and sometimes even lucky things—are happening to a lot of people, perhaps in ways they can't recognize in the moment. Maybe an understanding of our story (including my many, many mistakes) will give you a fresh perspective of your own unique story. After all, you can't produce opportunity, but you can prepare yourself to be ready for it if and when it comes.

But, if you really want to get down to brass tacks, mine is a story of luck, both in my personal life and in business.

Regardless, I can't deny that I have lived a very different and exceptional story on this earth—one that I don't deserve, but one that my family thinks you might enjoy.

A Mentor and His Maxims

There is so much that I look forward to sharing with you about many of the incredible people and experiences in my life, but to help you understand the way I'm going to do this, I must jump ahead a bit and introduce you to a key figure in my life: General Robert R. Neyland. General Neyland was one of the most accomplished and renowned football coaches of his era—and also one of my most respected mentors.

General Neyland was a native Texan born in Greenville in 1892. After graduating from high school, he entered Burleson Junior College in Greenville (a school that was shut down in 1930) and then spent a year at Texas A&M before being appointed to West Point. His father had hoped he would follow in his footsteps and become an attorney, but young Robert did not want to practice law. Rather, he was destined to train young men by putting them through a much different type of rigorous *practice*.

For the next three years at West Point, Neyland learned and excelled at military theory, knowledge, and discipline, but he also proved himself to be a standout all-around athlete. While he lettered in football both in 1914 (an undefeated season) and 1915, he was actually more widely known for his accomplishments on the baseball field and in the boxing ring.

Cadet Neyland was more than just a stellar athlete; he graduated near the top of his class in 1916, the year before the United States entered The Great War (WWI) already raging in Europe. Fresh out of the Academy, he was recruited to play professional baseball by the New York Giants, the Detroit Tigers, and the Philadelphia Athletics. However, as a skilled soldier possessing his own unique caliber of integrity and honor, Neyland refused to let other young men fight overseas while he played baseball. He turned down his pro offers and shipped out soon after graduation.

Neyland served with distinction in France during World War I, working with the Army Corp of Engineers. Near the end of the war, the Army reassigned him to train engineers at Fort Bliss, Texas. However, he was soon sent southward to join in the pursuit of Pancho Villa near the U.S.–Mexico border. His leadership acumen and attention to detail led to promotion after promotion until he became one of the youngest regimental commanders in the U.S. Army.

The Army then shipped him off to the Massachusetts Institute of Technology (MIT) for a year of postgraduate studies in civil engineering. Little did anyone know at the time that the knowledge he gained during this year of study would someday help him dream and design one of the most impressive and historically hallowed stadiums in all of college football.

After MIT, he returned to West Point, where he was appointed an aide to then-Superintendent General Douglas MacArthur. It was at West Point that Neyland first became involved in coaching various sports, including football. In the spring of 1925, he was assigned to the University of Tennessee as the Professor of Military Science and Tactics—and he also became an assistant football coach for the

Tennessee Volunteers (Vols). He was quickly promoted to position of Head Football Coach and Athletic Director by December of the same year. Over the next nine years with the Vols, Neyland led his football team to five undefeated seasons, including undefeated streaks of thirty-three and twenty-eight straight games!

In those days, every male student was required to take at least two years of Reserve Officers' Training Corps (ROTC), so the Department of Military Science and Tactics had a larger influential presence on campus and within the university structure. This also meant there were multiple high-ranking military officers teaching on the campus. Neyland remained connected to the military during this time, teaching and coaching until 1934, when he was called back into full-time active service.

> Let that sink in: Neyland's defense was so stout that no team scored a single point on them for an entire slate of regular season games—not even a field goal.

After serving in Panama for a year, he returned to Tennessee in 1936 as the Head Football Coach. His 1938 team went undefeated and was proclaimed National Champion by certain media outlets. (At that time, a consensus organization and system for ensuring an undisputed, unanimous champion had not yet been created.) The 1939 team not only went undefeated but was also the last team in college football history to hold all its opponents completely scoreless for an entire regular season.

Let that sink in: Neyland's defense was so stout that no team scored a single point on them for an entire slate of regular season games—not even a field goal. The 1940 team also remained undefeated. Then, in 1941, Uncle Sam called upon him yet again to join in a more important defense: that of our nation against our formidable foes overseas. During World War II, he served in China and India, supervising the transportation of materials through monsoons and over mountains, navigating critical supplies and resources across the Himalayas to troops commanded by General "Vinegar Joe" Stilwell.

Neyland was eventually awarded the Distinguished Service Medal and the Legion of Merit. He was also made a member of the Order of the British Empire. But when he retired from military service in 1946 with the rank of Brigadier General, he was ready to come home to Knoxville to resume coaching the Tennessee Volunteers for another seven years.

It was during *those* last seven years that my path crossed his.

Hopefully, this little history lesson will help you understand how significant it was for me that this overweight young man—*me*—was lucky enough to be coached by a living legend at such a formative moment. I'll talk much more about my years under General Neyland's leadership later in this book. For now, I want to use one of the General's most famous and practical tools as a framework for telling parts of my own story. He coined seven adages throughout his legendary career that, to this day, remain a solid roadmap for achieving victory on the football field. These are generally referred to as Neyland's Game Maxims, and they still hang in the Tennessee locker room in the stadium that now bears his name. Every week, all the players recite the maxims together as a hallowed tradition before taking the field to face their opponent, and really, to face *themselves*.

These are reminders of what it takes to best position oneself and one's team to win on the field of play, but, in my opinion, some of them can also be helpful in positioning oneself in life. Though there are modern versions that are slightly different in places, here are Neyland's Game Maxims close to their original form as he taught them to us on a weekly basis. I still know them by heart:

1. *The team that makes the fewest mistakes wins.*
2. *Play for and make the breaks. When one comes your way, SCORE.*
3. *If at first the game—or a break—goes against you, don't slow down or get rattled. Put on more steam.*

4. *Line and backs protect our kicker and passer. Line and ends rush their kicker and passer.*[2]
5. *Ball, oskie, cover, block, cut and slice, pursue, and gang tackle…for here is the WINNING EDGE.*
6. *Press the kicking game. Here is where the breaks are made.*
7. *Carry the fight to Alabama*[3] *and keep it there all afternoon.*

You may or may not be a Tennessee fan, but if you follow college football at all, my bet is that you've heard these before, probably as part of a pregame television feature. While it is a moving experience simply to hear all the players recite the maxims in unison, I actually know what it feels like to hear General Neyland himself lead the entire team in reciting them together.

There was nothing quite like seeing General Neyland write the maxims by hand on the locker room blackboard before each game.

These experiences and principles still profoundly affect me today—so much so that, over the years, I have developed my own set of twelve life maxims as something to pass down to my grandchildren. A few years back, my younger son, former Tennessee Governor Bill Haslam, asked me to memorialize these maxims by sharing them at a speaking engagement. I'm glad he did, because the process helped me really hone and express those things that have proven to be most important in my life.

Though no team will ever chant these maxims before "running through the T" at Neyland Stadium, I will be sharing and expounding upon them where they fit throughout the course of my story—and I will also dedicate an entire chapter to them later in this book. For now, I'll simply list them all here for reference.

---

2 "Line" in this sentence refers to offensive lineman, while "backs" refer to fullbacks and tailbacks. "Line" and "ends" in the second sentence refer to defensive lineman, defensive ends, and linebackers.

3 Many versions of this maxim read: "Carry the fight to 'our opponent' and keep it there all afternoon". However, since Alabama always was and will always be our biggest rival, I prefer to recite it this way.

My Life Maxims

1. **Christian Belief**

   Believe in the Trinity: the Father, the Son, and the Holy Spirit; the resurrection; and life everlasting. Worship regularly, study the Bible, and be united with Christ.

2. **Optimism**

   Optimists get things done! Positive attitudes always win!

3. **Humility and Kindness**

   Be humble, be kind, and always remember the less fortunate. It is always easy to be kind.

4. **Family First**

   Your family must always come first. Everything else pales in comparison.

5. **Politics**

   Get involved in the political process. Run for office and, if you don't, find candidates you like and raise money and work to get them elected. Who serves on the School Board is just as important as who represents us in the United States Senate.

6. **Set the Example and Change Is a Must**

   You must always set a good example. People will follow your example so make sure it is a good one. And remember, change is a positive and is your friend.

7. **Integrity**

   Always do the right thing. Always be faithful and accountable in every way.

8. **Keep It Simple**

   Leaders simplify things; they don't complicate things.

9. **Health, Exercise, Alcohol, and Drugs**

   Stay in shape. Work out, run, walk, ride a bicycle inside or outside, but whatever you do, make sure you have a good cardio program, watch your weight, and get plenty of sleep. I recommend not drinking at all, but if you do drink, never drink excessively. Never use illegal drugs, and gambling will only get you in trouble.

10. **Work Hard and Have a Purpose to Your Life**

    There is no substitute for hard work. Never let anyone outwork you. Remember, time is your most important asset, so working smart is just as important as working hard. And you must have a purpose in life.

11. **Passion**

    Be passionate in what you are doing, whether it's at work, working in the community, or at play.

12. **Give Back**

    We must give back! Luke 12:48 says, "To whom much is given, much is required." Give to your church, social causes, education, and the arts. It is your choice what you give to, but you must give back. The biblical tithe is 10 percent of your income, and that should be a minimum.

Their Takes and My Breaks

As I told you earlier, my family and friends have insisted that I write the details of my story, and I am honored by their request. However, this story would be nothing without them. So, several others will speak into the story in the Afterword As I sit here writing this, I'm not even sure what they will say; I have only asked them to be honest and share what is helpful, and I've instructed them not to simply pat me on the back. However, if they do so a little out of kindness, I suppose the right thing to do is to be grateful. But the point is that this is *our* story, so I thought you might want to hear *their* take and not just mine. I hope you will be enriched by the perspectives of the people who have enriched me the most.

Finally, for the sake of structure, I want to focus on General Neyland's second game maxim as a format for the first section, which follows the chronological details of our story in life and in business. The second maxim says, "Play for and make the breaks. When one comes your way, SCORE."

As I said, I've had some lucky breaks—events and occurrences that proved to be instrumental in the direction of my life and story. None of them had anything to do with my superior ability, intellect, or worthiness. The lucky breaks just *happened* to me, and I did my best—not always successfully—to apply General Neyland's second maxim, trying to make the most of what came my way.

To that end, the principle found in this second maxim—playing for breaks and trying to score if and when they come—is one of the key ways I will structure elements of our story in the pages ahead. Just as I have twelve life maxims, there are eight breaks that characterize the main narrative of my personal and business life. Many of these were seemingly small and fairly inconsequential in the moment, but that is the nature of life: it is rarely a series of big breaks.

The second maxim says, "Play for and make the breaks. When one comes your way, SCORE."

Most of what matters in real life is made up of the small things. I learned that from General Neyland on the field of play, just as I later learned it by serving in the military, serving my family as a husband and father, and serving my team members leading Pilot Company. If we can live life gratefully taking notice and faithfully making the most of the *small* things we can control and affect, we will look back on our experiences and be shocked at all the *big* things behind us we could never predict or even clearly see as they were happening. I want to invite you to look back with me at our story ... and especially at some of the incredible people who have affected me so deeply.

How did all this happen? Let me start by showing you the breaks that came my way.

SECTION I

THE BREAKS

The Timeline of Our Story

CHAPTER 2

THE BIG DEAL OF SMALL BEGINNINGS

From Pennsylvania to St. Petersburg: My First Big Break

I was born in Detroit, Michigan, on December 13, 1930. It was a Friday, but I can truthfully say that the old wives' tale about the "unlucky" Friday the 13th has certainly not been the case in my life. I've been extremely fortunate.

My father, James Arthur Haslam, was born on Prince Edward Island, Canada, in 1894. When he was twenty years old, my father went into the Canadian army. He was in active combat for more than two years, serving as a Company Commander in Princess Patricia's Canadian Light Infantry during World War I. After the war in the early 1920s, his family moved from Prince Edward Island to St. Paul, Minnesota. It was there that my father met my mother, Melitta Fry. Her family had lived in St. Paul for multiple generations. They married in 1922 and eventually had three children. I am the youngest, with two older sisters, Marie and Pat, both of whom are now deceased.

After World War I, my father followed in the footsteps of *his* father and began working in the insurance and real estate businesses. But when the stock market crashed in 1928, the business took such a hit that he left the family business and went to work for Studebaker Corporation in Detroit, which was where I was born. When I was one year old, Studebaker transferred him to Harrisburg, Pennsylvania, where he worked as a factory sales representative. He had a territory of dealers for whom he provided inventory.

Times were tough for my family during the Depression, as they were for most people. Today, you generally see cars being delivered to dealerships by big trucks on the highways, but back then, cars were usually delivered by train. My father would go down to the railroad yard, get a car from whatever load had just arrived, and drive it around to various dealers in his territory to find someone who'd take it off his hands. If he was able to make the sale, he would have someone at the dealership take him back to the railroad yard to pick up another car, and then he'd start the whole process again.

My father was an extremely hard worker, an ethic instilled in him from the military. In fact, even when he worked for Studebaker, he was still an Army man at heart. When World War II broke out, he immediately joined the U.S. Army with the rank of Major. He served from the time I was in seventh grade until I was a junior in high school, eventually being discharged as a Lieutenant Colonel. I was so proud of him. However, his absence meant that I didn't get to spend much time with him during most of my teenage years.

As you would suspect, he was always extremely disciplined and wanted *me* to become disciplined as well. When he left to go overseas in the Army, he said, "Now, do what your mother says. If she says, 'Clean your fingernails,' then you clean your fingernails!" He wanted me to learn how to work hard and carry myself with the dignity reflective of a military family. Later on, when I had the chance to play football at the University of Tennessee, my father was thrilled that I would be playing for General Neyland. It was the kind of environment and training my father most wanted me to experience—and he was right.

My father was gone most of the time when I was young and, by the time he came home from the service, I was on my way to college and then into the service myself. He died when I was twenty-two years old while I was in Basic Engineers Officer Training School at Fort Belvoir, Virginia. Looking back, I realize that I never got to know him that well. He was a good father, but I wish I could have had more time with him. I think this realization is what drove me to pursue relationships with my own kids when I became a father myself.

My mother, sisters, and I always had a good relationship. Mother was a wonderful person who always tried to do the right thing. She was also very active, something I think she passed on to me. She had excellent interpersonal skills and was a delight to speak with.

She also made me go to church—*no matter what.* I can remember a time in high school when one of my baseball games fell on Good Friday. It didn't matter how important the game was to our season or how important my role was to our team, there was no chance on God's green earth that I was going to be allowed to play in a baseball game on Good Friday. I didn't.

> It didn't matter how important the game was to our season or how important my role was to our team, there was no chance on God's green earth that I was going to be allowed to play in a baseball game on Good Friday.

Mother lived a rich, full life after my father died, staying active even throughout her last fifteen years when she was completely blind. She died at the age of eighty-two. I remain grateful to God for a good mother who taught me so many important things such as staying active and making the most of every second you've been granted on this earth.

Returning to my childhood story, we lived in the Harrisburg, Pennsylvania, area until 1938 when my father was transferred to Teaneck, New Jersey, for a year. When I was in fourth grade, he was transferred yet again, this time to the Philadelphia area. He went back into the Army during this time, and the rest of us stayed in Philadelphia until his return during my junior year at Lower Merion High School in Ardmore.

Lower Merion had stellar athletic programs (Kobe Bryant went directly to the NBA from this school), and I was fortunate enough to play football, basketball, and baseball. However, football was definitely my best sport. We had excellent football teams and, being a bigger boy, I played both ways as an offensive tackle and defensive tackle. I was lucky enough to be a varsity starter as a sophomore and as a junior.

But as my senior year approached, I faced the first real event that changed the course of my future life. You can call this my *first break*. My father had heart problems and when he came home from the service, he and my mother decided it was time to retire and move to St. Petersburg, Florida, where the climate was more suited for his health issues. This meant a major move for our family. Most people today would hardly consider making a child leave his home, friends, and everything he knew and loved right before his senior year; back then, however, you just did what your parents told you to do. They said we were moving to Florida, and we moved to Florida. End of story.

> I am so grateful I was as big as I was, because it eventually allowed me to have some of the most important experiences of my life playing football for the University of Tennessee.

I'm so glad we did, though, because what seemed difficult at the time would prove to be one of the first big breaks in my life. Fortunately, the football coach from Lower Merion, Dick Mattis, wrote a recommendation letter for me to John Sexton, the football coach at St. Petersburg High School. When we moved to Florida, I was welcomed into St. Petersburg High—and into the football program—with open arms.

But the real reason this was such a huge moment in my story might surprise you: it was literally the weather. I said earlier that I was a "bigger" boy, but the truth is, I was a *fat* boy. Yes, I understand it isn't popular to use an expression like this these days, but the only person I aim to offend here is myself, so I guess it's okay to call it like I see it. I had always been a big kid, and I had grown into a fairly overweight teenager.

Obviously, the weather is quite different in Florida than it is in Pennsylvania, so when I put on those heavy pads and began practicing in the blistering heat and humidity of a Southern climate, pounds of fat melted off and were replaced with pounds of muscle. I became much faster and developed much more stamina, which made me into a much better football player all around.

I used to be one of the biggest guys around, which is why many people called me *Big Jim*. Being *big* in the 1950s was a *big deal* for football teams, because players were generally a lot smaller back then. The size of a team's players not only greatly affected how many wins and losses it would have; it also affected the number that each player was assigned. These days, players are generally given numbers that reflect their positions. Offensive ends are usually in the eighties, tackles in the seventies, guards in the sixties, and centers and linebackers in the fifties. But when I started playing football, you were assigned a number based upon your size. When I played at Lower Merion High School, the team's numbers went from 10 to 53. I was number 53. When I moved to St. Petersburg, the numbers ranged from 10 to 46. I was number 46. For most of my youth, I was the biggest kid—and I had the jersey to prove it.

Though I first played organized football in junior high school, my size benefited me the most in high school. Back then, it was a big deal to break two hundred pounds. I will never forget the morning I woke up to see the number 200 on my scale. (I still weigh every day because I like to be attentive to as many aspects of my health and fitness as possible.) I was only a sophomore when I hit 200 pounds. I was so excited that I called the football coach at home to inform him of the news. I am so grateful I was as big as I was, because it eventually allowed me to have some of the most important experiences of my life playing football for the University of Tennessee.

So what had seemed to be a difficult moment—moving to Florida for my senior year—proved to be one of my greatest advantages. Little did I know that becoming a better football player would be the first of many important dominoes to fall in my life.

Our line coach at St. Petersburg High School was Gerald Hendricks. Gerald was a native of Knoxville and had played for the University of Tennessee. From the get-go, Coach Hendricks urged me to take a look at Tennessee. In fact, he and I, along with another teammate named Otto Frudenberger, went to Knoxville to watch the Tennessee–Vanderbilt game in 1948. Tennessee won that game by a score of 14 to 7. I suppose the fact that I remember the score means the trip made quite an impression on me.

I enjoyed the experience immensely, but I was also still planning to keep all my options open. I took visits to Clemson and Duke, as well as the University of Florida. Florida was not a very good football program in those days, so they didn't really make the cut. Army always had the best football teams in the mid-1940s, and I briefly considered going to West Point, but I found out I would have to go to prep school for a year and that wasn't the path I wanted to take. I also briefly looked at Alabama, a school that hadn't yet been graced with the legendary Coach Paul "Bear" Bryant. I was mulling over all these options, but everything changed when I met General Robert R. Neyland.

Our first meeting was anything but orthodox. I was playing in a basketball game at our school. At halftime, our coach, John Axton, told me that General Neyland was sitting up in the stands watching our game. I looked up into the stands and saw him for the first time. He was an impressive looking man, but little did I know he also had a certain way about him that would greatly influence the daunting decisions before me.

After the game, General Neyland came over and said, "Son, let's go have a piece of pie and talk." I was more than happy to oblige him, so we went to a place called The Poinsettia Restaurant. I guess you could say that hanging out in a little café with Warren Buffett wasn't the first time I have shared a humble meal with a humble legend. General Neyland talked to me for a long time about my family, my future, and what I wanted to pursue in life. He was an impressive and confident man, and, though a little intimidating, he seemed interested in my well-being. Needless to say, after that night and that piece of pie, I was pretty sure I was going to the University of Tennessee.

This was the *second break* of my story. If we hadn't moved to Florida, and if there hadn't been an assistant coach there with Tennessee connections, I never would have had the opportunity to come to the University of Tennessee...and all the great things God has given to me, our family, and our company might never have happened.

Freshman Mistakes and More Breaks

After graduating from high school in 1948, I made the trip to Knoxville by train and arrived at the L&N Railroad station. No one met me there, so I asked for directions and walked with my own bag from the railroad depot to the campus to officially begin my student career at the University of Tennessee.

Though I had to begin worrying about classes and studying, my greatest concern was football and life with my new teammates. It is interesting to note that in those days, there were no scholarship limits. So when I showed up for the first day of practice, I was joined by eighty-eight other freshmen. Needless to say, it was going to be a grueling process to determine who would stay (and survive). Most players would end up quitting or transferring to other schools to seek playing time—after sitting out an entire season, of course. Of those eighty-eight freshmen who dressed out for that inaugural practice, only about twelve of us ended up graduating from the University of Tennessee.

Freshmen were not eligible to play on the varsity squad back then. Paul "Bear" Bryant was coaching at Kentucky at the time, and he and General Neyland decided to pull together a freshman game between our two schools. We loaded up on buses and rode to Lexington for our first real action as players being coached by two football heavyweights.

There was another hidden purpose behind this matchup. Obviously, there was no transfer portal in those days, so anyone who played in this game would be ineligible to transfer to another school without sitting out for a year. It was a way to keep the incoming freshmen around for at least a year to see who could be developed into quality contributors. As you'd expect, that game between our two freshman squads—merely two weeks into our college careers—was *ugly*. Kentucky won 7–0. The game was fraught with mistakes, but no mistake was ever wasted by General Neyland. He used each moment on the field, good and bad (and, as freshmen most of them *were* bad), to begin teaching us how to persevere through them so that, one day, we could be able to minimize the mistakes through discipline, intention, and the right kind of championship thinking.

We began learning his maxims from day one, which is probably why I can still recite them from memory today. The first one dealt with exactly what we were experiencing the most: blunders. General Neyland knew the place to begin our instruction was with realizing and internalizing the fact that the team that makes the fewest mistakes will win.

This lesson never left me, even long after my college football days were done. When you think about it, General Neyland never said you aren't going to make any mistakes. In life, it's going to happen. You *will* fumble and stumble, but you don't have to grumble. Mistakes are life's most effective teachers and, if you never make them, you will also never do anything worthwhile. But, if you don't learn from them, you certainly can make *too many* mistakes and forfeit many good breaks that might come your way.

Once you understand this, you can be free to learn from your mistakes so you don't continue repeating them over and over again. After all, much of winning in life is really about minimizing mistakes. This taught us that we had to work hard, become active learners, exercise personal discipline, and ultimately work together towards a common goal, sharing in the collective mission to minimize our shortcomings and maximize our strengths. We learned that it was good when *one of us* did these things; but from a football perspective, we were nearly unstoppable when *all of us* did them intentionally.

I believe this same principle rings true in family and in business.

So again, my second big break was most definitely having the opportunity to go to the University of Tennessee. During my time there, I played on a national championship football team, which was a life-changing experience. But even more importantly, I met incredible people who have deeply impacted my life, many of whom are still the closest of friends today. Though I will more fully unpack some of these stories a bit later, for now, you should know that I also met my first wife, Cynthia, at the University of Tennessee.

We began learning his maxims from day one, which is probably why I can still recite them from memory today.

I suppose that it's hard to measure just how big little beginnings can be. We tend to want to boil life down to its major events, which often causes us to miss the fact that very few events in life are really *minor*, even if they seem to be so at the time. Think about those moments in your own life when you chose Path A instead of Path B— and from that one seemingly small decision, a million other events unfolded from jobs, to moves, to marriages, to children, and so on.

My second break most definitely falls into this category. From Detroit to Philadelphia to St. Petersburg, I had no idea at the time how fateful my move to East Tennessee would ultimately prove to be in my life. God certainly knew, but He would only allow time to tell the full story.

I learned so much during these early years. It felt like I was drinking fun, knowledge, and discipline directly from a fire hose. And, though it was difficult at times and I was only a kid, I think I somehow recognized in the moment that these experiences would ultimately prove to be some of the most fun and important of my entire life.

I majored in business and joined the Sigma Chi fraternity, both of which directly affected my future. However, most of what I learned during college came from my time on the football team. Our first game of the 1950 season was against Mississippi State. We lost the game 7–0 to an inferior team. This was something General Neyland wasn't used to and, honestly, something he would not tolerate. He didn't panic, though, which helped us keep our heads too. We stayed the course, learning to practice and think like hard workers and winners for the purpose of seeing this kind of thinking become second nature. It must have worked because, after that initial loss, we won the next twenty games in a row!

The next season, we left no doubt and won the undisputed national championship in 1951, winning all ten games in the regular season.

That stellar record didn't help our national ranking that year, I'm afraid. Back then, the national champion was determined after the last regular game of the season by a vote of the Associated Press. There was no coaches' polls or postseason consensus voting. By the end of the season, since we had lost the first game, we ended up being ranked fourth behind Oklahoma, Army, and Texas. But if you really break it down, things were much more interesting than they first appear because of the way the final games played out. We beat Kentucky in the next-to-last game of the season by a score of 7–0. We then went to the Cotton Bowl in the postseason and faced third-ranked Texas, which proved to be one of the most memorable games in Tennessee football history. We emerged victorious by a score of 20–14.

When all was said and done, we had beaten the third-ranked team while Kentucky, which we had also beaten, went to the Sugar Bowl and beat Oklahoma, the top-ranked team. In the meantime, Army and Navy played each other a week later after these national rankings came out—and wouldn't you know it, Navy beat second-ranked Army. All that being said, in today's world, Tennessee would have ended up being the top-ranked team in 1950!

The next season, we left no doubt and won the undisputed national championship in 1951, winning all ten games in the regular season. We went to the Sugar Bowl during the postseason to face the second-ranked Maryland Terrapins. Sadly, as the national champions, we lost our bowl game. If you were to think of national championships like we do today, we would have won it all in 1950, not 1951. Regardless, these were historic seasons in Tennessee football history, but they were also some of the most incredible moments of my young life.

One of the greatest honors of my life came in 1952 when I was voted Captain of the University of Tennessee football team. Being a captain of a football team was a lot different back then than it is today. I was elected Captain the Monday after the Vanderbilt game and, from that moment, remained the Captain for the whole calendar year, technically overlapping multiple seasons.

The role of Captain was not a token position that simply meant being the first one to practice, leading drills, or walking out to the center of the field for the coin toss, though the Captain certainly did all of those things. This was a legitimate position of leadership and authority that came with a host of duties and responsibilities. Above all else, the Captain was the liaison between General Neyland and the players, especially in matters of discipline. It was his job to keep up with the players and know what was going on in their lives. If a player got into trouble, the Captain had to decide whether or not the matter should be taken up the ladder to the coaches or handled by him. In this, the Captain was a student who was tasked with leading—and disciplining—other students. In this way, we were expected to look out for one another never passively waiting for "adults" to show up and enforce our boundaries.

Yes, we were technically adults ourselves, but we still engaged in all the hijinks that typically accompanies college life. Some of the stories I could tell are pretty funny; others are much more serious. In fact, I could embarrass quite a few people by sharing those details, so it's probably best that I don't!

Regardless, early in my life, I was expected to take responsibility for my peers. Looking back, owning that responsibility was a tall task, but I am so thankful someone required me to do it. When young people are given more than just an education, but also responsibility to look out for others and not just themselves, deeply meaningful foundations are laid for their future and for the futures of those around them. They become leaders the right way: by serving the interests of those around them. The bottom line was that I wasn't expected to just look out for myself, but also for those on my team ... for better or for worse.

Campus Life and Campus Love

The life of a football player was much different in the 1950s than it is today. Most modern collegiate football players are not a part of a fraternity, but when I played, most of us had pledged and were a part of Greek society on campus.

Today the University of Tennessee is a huge, sprawling campus with more than thirty thousand students coming and going to countless classes, labs, practices, offices, dining facilities, athletic training sessions, study groups, events, and a host of other things happening in many places. The campus is made up of so many beautiful buildings that it looks more like a small city than a college. But it wasn't like this in 1950—not by a long shot.

There were roughly five thousand students and faculty on campus, which was large in terms of acreage but not in terms of facilities. Most of our classes were held in Ayres Hall, the iconic building usually featured in commercials for the university. It is a beautiful Gothic Revival-style building that was completed in 1921, and its tall clock tower features a checkerboard pattern that has been replicated in the end zone of the stadium for years.

Ayres Hall stands atop "The Hill," a historic sight that now houses many other buildings. Among the crowded landscape, Ayres remains the focal point and the most recognizable university building. During the Civil War, The Hill was a key fortified position southeast of Fort Sanders that played an important role in the Union defense against an ultimately unsuccessful Confederate siege, led by Lieutenant General James Longstreet, to control Knoxville and its key railroad supply lines.

Over the years, The Hill has always been a kind of "rite of passage" for Tennessee students who have trudged up her steep terrain in rain, sleet, and snow. Of course, today there is a nice walking bridge that lets you stroll straight to the top with no sweating, climbing, or discomfort.

While Ayres Hall was the center of our educational experience, the football stadium was the center of our lives. When an athlete today is extraordinarily motivated to practice and improve, it might be said that he or she "lives on the practice field" or "lives at the stadium." In my day, however, we *literally* lived in the stadium, mainly because we slept there every night in various rooms and bunks throughout what is still the lower part of the structure today. Really zealous Tennessee fans might say that Neyland Stadium is a second home to them; but for four years of my life, it was my *actual* home.

It was called Shields–Watkins Field back then, the name still ascribed to the playing surface today. Just like Ayres Hall, the first version of the stadium was finished in 1921. At the time of its completion, it was not even a fraction of the size of the largest football stadium in Tennessee, which was Dudley Field at Vanderbilt University in Nashville.

As I said before, it was the gifted engineering mind of General Neyland—taking full advantage of his educational exile to MIT—that spearheaded the vision of what the stadium could ultimately become, which is one of the largest football stadiums in the country, once boasting a capacity of over 108,000 people. Over the years, every expansion to the facility has been influenced by Neyland's original plans. He was that far ahead of his time.

When I was a student there, the stadium was much smaller, but it was still larger than life to those of us who called it home. It was where we slept, ate, and practiced. Several of my teammates were also Sigma Chis, including the All-American tailback and one of my closest friends, Hank Lauricella. We would wake up in the stadium and walk to the fraternity house for meetings and events. These two places were where most of the daily events of our lives occurred.

An incredible camaraderie existed among the football players, as well as our fraternity brothers. We were all best buddies and basically inseparable. Part of the reason for our closeness was the fact that General Neyland did not allow us to have cars at school. This meant our whole lives were tethered to the campus.

We often walked together down to Cumberland Avenue, the main road that runs through campus, to buy something from the drugstore that used to sit on the corner where the Student Union building stands today. There were many places to eat and hang out up and down this strip. We frequented The T Room (T for Tennessee) fairly often, but our favorite place was Byerly's Cafeteria, where we would meet between classes for sweet rolls and coffee (though I didn't partake of coffee then or now).

Even though we were mostly confined to the campus, we still felt such a sense of freedom. Some of the guys would do some pretty crazy things; in fact, Doug Atkins, probably the best player ever to don a jersey for Tennessee, was known to do some wildly funny things, which you can read about in various articles written since his passing. I'll leave it to you to find those stories for yourself. I guess you could say that, as Captain, I'm still covering for him.

Much of our fun wasn't stereotypical college shenanigans; it was just experiencing the freedom of trying new things. One day, we were all hanging out in Byerly's when our friend Bob Campbell decided he might want to go to law school. We talked for a few minutes about it, and the idea seemed to "gee and haw" with him (a Southern way of saying that it sat well with him), so he just got up and walked across the street to the law building to apply. Soon afterward, he was accepted into law school— just like that. Little decisions were producing such huge outcomes, which I suppose is true of anyone in this stage of life.

For us, the campus was the beating heart of this exciting life. Of course, we weren't the only ones on campus; there were girls there too! Since the student population was so much smaller, everyone pretty much knew everyone else in some form or fashion, especially if you were in a fraternity or sorority. The Greek life provided ample opportunities to ask eligible girls on dates.

During my junior year, I asked a certain smart and beautiful Delta Delta Delta member named Cynthia Allen to go with me to a Sigma Chi party. She accepted and we ended up dating for the next two years until our marriage in 1953, the year after I graduated. Marrying Cynthia was an integral part of the break that came my way when I came to Tennessee—she made my life so much better in ways I could never describe.

With college and football behind me, I was entering the next season of life as a married man. I now had a wife to protect and care for, just as I had been tasked with protecting and caring for the team as Captain. Of course, if things got bad enough with the team, I would take matters to General Neyland. In this way, I had a responsibility, but there was also a strong safety net to keep me protected. That safety net helped train me as a husband and a father as well.

All told, the entire process of college and football was focused on training us to be men who would take ownership and accountability for ourselves, our families, our friends, and our country. This intentional education to shift our focus off ourselves and onto others was not just a wonderful experience but also instrumental in shaping the way I instinctively began to think about life, leadership, and legacy. It affected the lenses through which I see family, teams, and the need to lead by serving. The lessons weren't always easy, and I haven't always applied them well, but these experiences most definitely laid a foundation during the most formative time of my life.

I soon would need to apply these lessons—this time for something much more important than winning a football game.

CHAPTER 3

OCEANS APART

A Different Kind of Uniform

I MAY HAVE BEEN A MEMBER OF THE FOOTBALL TEAM AND A FRATER-
nity, but my coaches and leaders took a much deeper interest in me
beyond just athletics or academics. They felt a responsibility to pay
forward what had been done for them by helping us make connections
and take the next steps, even when those steps no longer had anything
to do with them directly. I suppose they cared more about our personal
growth than what they could get out of us for themselves.

I think the general attitude of "giving back" was really reinforced
in me during these years. Though I had been the team Captain, I was
trained never to revel in the mere title or exposure of the position. Being
Captain was a job that entailed looking out for others—and not just in
matters of football. This was just the way it worked. We looked out for
one another from the day we started classes to the day that we graduated…and, in many cases, for many years afterward. That's why some of
my friends from college are still my closest friends today.

I was seventeen years old when I came to University of Tennessee.
When I graduated in December 1952, the Korean War was raging. Keep
in mind that World War II had ended only about seven years earlier,
so the world and all of us in it were still feeling the shockwaves from

that war. Many young men were conscripted to continue serving their country in Korea, although any soldier who had served in World War II did not have to register for the current draft.

Understanding the current state of world affairs, General Neyland had been looking out for us long before we could comprehend the extent of his influence. He had been working hard to mold us into responsible men, not just talented football players. Knowing many of us would be bound for the service after graduation, every male student entered ROTC. Again, ROTC was compulsory for the first two years, but most of us remained in the program all four years. As a result, when I graduated, I was commissioned as a Second Lieutenant in the U.S. Army—and, on February 1, 1953, I reported to active duty at Fort Belvoir, Virginia.

> He had been working hard to mold us into responsible men, not just talented football players.

This was such a fascinating time in my life. I have always felt that, in terms of opportunity, being born in the United States is like winning the lottery. I don't mean to imply there are no opportunities elsewhere in the world or that no one in the U.S. has ever faced difficult circumstances, inequality, or injustice. I simply mean that, by and large, the statistical probability of being able to face and overcome whatever challenges are before you is higher for someone born here than for someone born into communist China or North Korea, especially in those early postwar years. So while I know our country isn't perfect, I have always felt it my highest honor to serve and protect the values and freedoms we do have and in which we continue to grow.

The first item of business for me at Fort Belvoir was a basic engineering officers training course; it lasted three months. While that was a fairly long training and I had also been through multiple years of ROTC, those of us who went through this process were still *green* in terms of military knowledge and experience, even though we were officers.

Why did I enter the Corps of Engineers? After all, I wasn't an engineer and didn't have an engineering background. Like many of my decisions back then, it was because of General Neyland. He'd been in the Corps of Engineers, and that's what he had encouraged all of us to do as well. So even though I didn't have an engineering background, I found myself serving with the engineers. And I wasn't alone—there were several of us from The University of Tennessee who were there together at Fort Belvoir—more on that soon.

Pigskin for Uncle Sam

In those days, each of the major military bases had a football team. When I finished my first round of training, they assigned me and a few others to Special Services, which entailed being in charge of the field house and helping out with matters related to athletics until the football season started.

When the season finally came, I had the honor not only of playing football for my country, but also doing so alongside some familiar faces. The most recognizable player on our team was the All-American Hank Lauricella, a fellow University of Tennessee Volunteer—and one of my greatest friends—who graduated with me in 1952. Another Tennessee player on our team was a great lineman named Bill "Pug" Pearman. Truth be told, we had a number of solid players, including George Morris from Georgia Tech who went on to play for the San Francisco 49ers and Bob Shemonski from Maryland who had played against us in the Sugar Bowl in 1952.

But probably the most surprising character on our team never put on football pads at all. The coach was none other Al Davis, who later became famous in professional football as a coach and team owner. I was only twenty-two years old at the time, and our coach was an *elderly* twenty-three.

Most of the guys on our team were officers, which was probably a testament to the trend in college football in those days to encourage players to enter ROTC. This also meant most of us were Second Lieutenants—*very green* Second Lieutenants. Strangely enough, Al Davis was only a Private First Class (PFC) and yet, somehow, he was our coach. We never quite figured out how that happened, but there we were: a team of officers taking "orders" from a Private.

Playing for Al Davis for almost a year was an experience I'll never forget. Of course, none of us knew he would go on to great heights. He became a professional football coach and eventually became the owner of the Oakland Raiders. As the mastermind who brought together the AFL and the NFL to form one cohesive National Football League, he is considered to be one of the most influential people in football history. But back in 1953, he was just an ambitious twenty-three-year-old coach trying to keep the rest of us in check.

Our team was called the Engineers, and we played the teams from other bases, which were also known by their respective branches of service. One week, we were slated to play the Quartermaster Corps from Fort Lee, and both teams shared the field for practice the day before the game. Afterward, our two teams hung out and had fun together.

Surprisingly, I had several buddies from Tennessee on the Fort Lee team. One of them called us over and said, "Hey, we got a guy here who can stand on fifty-yard line and throw the football into the end zone." Nowadays, there are lots of guys who can throw it that far, but it was very much a novelty back then. We said it wasn't possible, so the challenge was accepted.

One of the players yelled to another, "Hey, Willie, come here!" Over walks a stout young man in fatigues. He knew what they wanted him to do and, sure enough, he took the football and hurled a perfect spiral straight into the end zone.

It turned out that "Willie" was none other than baseball legend Willie Mays!

On game day, both teams came out of the same tunnel at the same time. The Fort Lee team had a player named Mike McCormick who went on to play for the Browns, and was eventually inducted into the NFL Hall of Fame as one of the all-time greatest tackles who ever played.

As we were coming out of the tunnel, Mike looked at me and said, "Haslam, this is service football. I say we just go half-speed."

Since General Neyland wasn't lurking nearby and we were all on the same "team" in terms of serving our country, it sounded like a good idea to me, so I replied, "Great! Let's do it!"

I had every intention of going half-speed, but when we got out there on the field, I found the competition from Fort Lee was significantly more stout than I expected. Instinctively, I ended up playing the absolute best I could just to keep up. All told, Mike McCormick outplayed me badly. At the end of the game, I was huffing and puffing as we walked off the field. Mike strolled up beside me, put his arm around me, and said, "Say Jim, we fooled 'em, didn't we?"

I laughed and agreed without trying to look too winded. He never knew that his *half-speed* was more than my *full-speed* could handle.

It turned out that "Willie" was none other than baseball legend Willie Mays!

The last game of the year was a Thanksgiving Day matchup against the Quantico Marines, which we lost. It was only the second time we had done so that season, as our final record was 8–2. We went back to Fort Belvoir on Monday after the holiday—and that was the day many of us received our orders to be deployed to Korea.

It was a memorable holiday, to say the least; we had lost the big game, and I was headed overseas.

The Hard (and Best) Way

It was December of 1953, and Cynthia was pregnant with our first child. I had my orders for deployment, but I wasn't supposed to report for about a month. This allowed me to spend Christmas with Cynthia and to see some of our family before leaving. On January 1, 1954, I reported to Fort Lewis in Washington and, by the middle of the same month, I arrived in Korea.

Though I didn't realize it at the time, this was definitely my *third break*. By this time, an armistice had been signed between North and South Korea, so I was not engaged in active combat. Ours was a peacekeeping mission. Even so, things were still tenuous. We were on the front lines of the Cold War—the epic struggle between the Soviet Union, with its constant attempt to spread communism to other parts of the world, and the United States' efforts to thwart those plans and help establish and preserve democracy instead. I know things were more complicated than this, but, for where I was in my life, it was pretty black and white...just like our televisions.

> He looked me square in the eye and said, "Son, if you can be a Captain for General Neyland's football team, then you can be a Company Commander."

I was assigned as the Executive Officer to the Headquarters Company, 1169th Combat Engineer Group. I had only been there for a few months when it became apparent that the Company Commander's alcohol abuse was causing major problems. To my surprise, the Group Commander, Colonel Frank E. Stevenson, called me in one day and said, "Lieutenant Haslam, I want you to be the new Company Commander."

"Well, Colonel Stevenson, sir," I replied, "I really don't know that much about the army. I'm not sure it would be the best move for these men."

He looked me square in the eye and said, "Son, if you can be a Captain for General Neyland's football team, then you can be a Company Commander."

That was that. I now was a Company Commander at the age of twenty-three. For the next nine months, I was in charge of the livelihood of one hundred and fifty men. I learned so much during this time.

It wasn't easy, but it was one of the most important experiences of my life. I had to lead by setting the example. The Company Commander was the first person to face a crisis and the last person to eat. In terms of understanding what leadership really is, nothing else prepared me quite as much at this experience.

This season was filled with challenges and problems, but honestly, each of these were also opportunities to grow. The truth was, I knew very little about running an engineer combat company. However, I was fortunate to have Sergeant Caldwell and Sergeant Landry under my command. One of them was the First Sergeant of the company, and the other was a Company Supply Sergeant. They were both leather-skinned veterans who had been in the Army for more than twenty years. They had both been involved in heavy combat during World War II and Korea before the ceasefire. Needless to say, these guys knew what they were doing, and their experiences were a huge help for their young commander who didn't.

It took me a little while to figure out that, even though I was their superior officer, it was okay that they knew more than me regarding what to do in certain situations. Their wisdom and experience were not just additional luxuries; I discovered that I absolutely *had* to have them in order to take good care of my men.

By the same token, they had to respect me, which they did. This was a lesson I learned early on in life: if you're going to be a leader, you have to make sure you are surrounded by the right people. And then you have to get out of their way and let them do their thing. The goal is not to do everything yourself, but rather to help others utilize their abilities in serving the bigger picture. Yes, they still have to respect your leadership, but that respect must be *earned*. Leadership means empowering others and entrusting them with the parts of the mission only they can accomplish.

I was a twenty-three-year-old kid leading career soldiers who were in their forties, but that's what leadership calls for sometimes. It didn't just make me a better leader but, also a much, much better person. I had a front-row seat to one of life's most important lessons: it's not just about me.

From the football field to the field of battle, this truth continually beckons leaders to something higher and better than improving their own reputation or advancement—if they are only willing to listen. Of course, I was not yet able to *fully* realize all these things as they were happening, but a lifetime of reflection has shown me this season was another one of God's greatest gifts to me, teaching me (the hard way) what it means to pursue humility—not because you want people to think you're humble, but because it actually is the best way to believe and live. Consequently, it is also what is best for those around you, including your family, team, church, company, or platoon.

> From the football field to the field of battle, this truth continually beckons leaders to something higher and better than improving their own reputation or advancement—if they are only willing to listen.

So much was happening in Korea during the time I was there, but a lot was happening back home as well. I was growing as a leader, but my family was also literally growing as Cynthia was due to give birth at any time. Obviously, this was long before the advent of the Internet and cell phones, so communication was much different. I found out that Jimmy was born when I received a telegram one week after his birth that simply said, "Boy. 8 pounds. Mother and baby both fine." Even though the news was not communicated in real time, I couldn't have been more excited.

I was a dad.

I was so fortunate that my news from home was the best kind, but everyone in my company wasn't always so fortunate. As the Company Commander, when news came in for a certain soldier about a tragedy that had occurred back home, it was my job to tell them. I was a young man myself, but, in those moments when I was sitting with a crying solider who had just found out he lost his mom or dad, I felt years older. I grew up quickly.

I had come to Tennessee as a seventeen-year-old boy. Now, six years later, through many experiences and influences with coaches, friends, and leaders, I was about to leave Korea and come home something else entirely. I had become a man, complete with all the responsibilities the role entails. It was time to take care of my growing family. And it was time to seek out what might be next after college, football, and the Army.

CHAPTER 4

LAUNCHING OUT

Coming Home

In November 1954, I was still in Korea and suddenly, I had a lot on my mind. I was two months away from coming home, and it was becoming increasingly apparent that I had no idea what I was supposed to do next to provide for my wife and little boy who would be almost one year old by the time I got home.

It might sound strange to say, but, between football and the Army, I came home very prepared for life in business. I just didn't know what that business might be. There was a certain mindset to the season of life I was about to exit that felt different from the one I was about to enter. In those days, the next steps on the path of adolescence and young adulthood usually seemed obvious, even if you had to be bold in making them. For me, these steps had always just appeared before me.

I would not have gone to college without a football scholarship. Again, I was the first in my family to ever attend—let alone graduate from—college. Then, after graduation, Uncle Sam made sure that I knew exactly what to do next by providing me an all-expense paid, year-long trip to Korea. Everything had been laid out for me up to this point, but now, the next steps toward my future brought with them an uncertainty I had never experienced.

So during my last few months in Korea, I began writing to specific people back home about what I might be able to do. I wrote to General Neyland, with whom I had stayed in contact and who was still my mentor. I also wrote to Howard Lumsden, who was in charge of a placement service for the university. He helped graduates make inroads and find networks for possible job opportunities.

General Neyland knew exactly what he wanted me to do. It was the same thing he wanted *all* of his former players to do: coach high school football. It made sense because coaching had meant so much to him. I think it was his way of continuing the tradition of brotherhood, camaraderie, and the disciplined training of young men for football and life. If more of his former players coached, it would help high school players become more prepared to play football at the next level the "right" way. Obviously, this also created a vast network of high school coaches motivated to help General Neyland recruit the best players to the University of Tennessee, so it made sense on all sides.

In my case, the only things that didn't make sense about coaching high school football were the timing and the pay. When I finally made it home from Korea, General Neyland gave me the information for a couple of high school football coaching jobs—and with his reference, I could pretty much have my pick. I reached out to several of them by phone and, in each case, the pay was only $350 a month. This would have been an average middle-class salary in those days, certainly nothing to write home about. Furthermore, even though they wanted me to start coaching in April for spring conditioning with the players, none of the schools could actually start paying me until classes started again in September.

With a family to take care of, I just couldn't afford to spend almost six months working for free, so I turned them all down and began looking elsewhere. Considering my love of football and the camaraderie of teams, coaching was a career I think I would have enjoyed immensely. If the timing had been different, you might be reading a different book altogether … or, perhaps, no book at all.

With my coaching career permanently sidelined, Howard Lumsden continued his work on helping me find other opportunities. He really came through, tracking down two possible jobs. The first was selling television advertising spots on a local TV station in Knoxville. The other was a long shot at best: a small oil company in the tiny town of LaFollette, Tennessee, about thirty miles northwest of Knoxville, was looking for a wholesale salesman who would also scout out locations for new gas stations.

The TV station scheduled me for an interview on a Wednesday, and it went very well. They expressed an interest in hiring me. The job paid $375 a month, which was more than the coaching positions. I asked them for a just a day or two to think about it, and they said to let them know by Friday.

I went home that night and talked everything over with Cynthia. To her, it seemed to be a no-brainer. "Aren't you going to take that job?" she asked. "It's right here in Knoxville, and it pays better than the others." She was right. The situa-tion would have put me squarely in a solid position right in the commu-nity we most wanted to be in. But there was something inside of me that had trouble accepting the position, something you'll probably laugh at.

> General Neyland knew exactly what he wanted me to do. It was the same thing he wanted **all** of his former players to do: coach high school football.

"Well," I said. "I'm really just not sure that television is going to make it."

Like I said at the start of this book, I've never claimed to be the smartest, only one of the luckiest. My reasoning for doubting the future of television may be hard to fathom today, considering its proliferation throughout every part of society, but things were very different back in 1954. There were only two television stations located in Knoxville: an NBC and a CBS affiliate. You could also pick up an ABC station from out of town if you positioned a TV's rabbit-ear antennae *just right*. And obviously, the whole world you'd see on a television screen was black and white. The bottom line was that the whole television industry was still very much in its infancy, and I didn't feel comfortable putting all my professional eggs into that particular basket.

I turned down the job and turned my attention to a little gas station chain in LaFollette. Believe it or not, that would turn out to be my *fourth break.*

Setting Sail

I drove to LaFollette to meet with a man named Sam Claiborne, the owner of Fleet Oil. Fleet was an independent oil company that operated about twenty gas stations in Tennessee and Kentucky.

Back then, you had the big major oil companies, most of which still exist today, including Exxon (which was called Esso in those days), Amoco, Gulf, BP, Chevron, Shell, Conoco, and Phillips. These major companies marketed their services through dealers. In addition to selling gas, these dealers offered repairs, lubrications, and other services. These companies also had the advantage of taking major oil company credit cards, which were some of the only credit cards that existed in those days. Independent or "cut-rate"oil companies sold only gasoline and didn't offer any of these additional services. They also operated on cash and didn't have the benefit of the credit cards, so they had to cut their prices to compete with the larger companies.

If the major companies were selling their fuel at 29.9 cents per gallon, the independents sold theirs at 27.9 cents per gallon. If the big guys sold at 31.9 cents, the independents sold at 29.9 cents. In those days, it was a big factor and a big opportunity for profit and growth, and that's exactly the business Fleet Oil was in.

Sam and I hit it off in our first meeting, and he offered me the job. When I inquired about the compensation, he asked, "How much do you want?"

I've turned down $350 and $375 per month, so I took a deep breath and said, "I'd like to have $400 per month, if you could make it work."

He looked me in the eyes and said, "Tell you what, I'll give you $5,000 a year." I was good enough in math to know that $5,000 a year was roughly $415 a month, which put me *ahead* of what I was asking for.

Before he could change his mind, I exclaimed, "I'll take it!" I started the job two weeks later. I had only been out of the Army for three weeks, and now I was starting a job that I believed could really become something special down the road. Sam hired me to help with the wholesale side of the business, as well as *location work*, helping scout out new locations that might be good fits for future gas stations.

Along with his brother, Sam owned *two* businesses: Fleet Oil and a construction company. I worked for Fleet Oil for a year, during which time my business relationship and friendship with Sam continued to grow. His brother was content with the way their businesses were going, but Sam wanted to expand. So Sam eventually started another company on his own called Sail Oil.

One day, Sam drove me to Pikeville, Kentucky, to show me the Sail station he had recently built there. That is where he told me that he wanted me to leave Fleet, run Sail Oil for him, and expand the company by building more stations. His gas stations were inexpensive to construct in those days because they were prefabricated buildings that Sam put together in a big barn in his backyard! With the cost of construction so low, he needed someone who could put serious energy into identifying and securing more sites to build.

It was a promotion for sure, but, if it *did* come with a raise, it was so small that I can't remember it. Sam did, however, offer me a small bit of ownership in the company if I wanted to put in a little of my own money. I said yes and soon scraped together (and borrowed) a small amount of money to invest into the company. With that, I was suddenly the head of Sail Oil.

Sam Claiborne taught me so much about trust and ownership in relationships and in business. Once, when I had only been working for him a little while, I was out doing location work when I found a potential spot in Roanoke, Virginia. It was a leased piece of property, and Sam agreed that it had potential, so we set a day to go look at it together.

It was a Monday when we set off on the six-hour drive from Knoxville to Roanoke. Because the property was held in a trust, we were supposed to meet with an attorney at his office in the downtown area around 2:00 p.m. to discuss details. However, we had stopped for lunch, and the drive had taken a little longer than we expected.

The prospective location-in-question was on the other side of Roanoke, and we were running out of time to get there and get back to the meeting by 2:00 p.m. When I started driving out to the location, Sam said, "Hey, if we go there first, we'll be late. Let's just go on downtown to his office." It seemed odd to me, but I did what he said. The next thing I knew, Sam signed the lease for the new location *site unseen*.

When we got in the elevator to leave, I asked him, "Have you ever seen this property before?"

"No," he replied.

"You mean, you just signed it because of what I said about it?"

> **"Yes, I did," he said. He paused for a moment, then continued, "Jim, you've got to get good people around you, and you've got to trust them."**

"Yes, I did," he said. He paused for a moment, then continued, "Jim, you've got to get good people around you, and you've got to trust them."

I was only twenty-five years old at the time, but this reinforced some of the same lessons I had learned from General Neyland and from my time in Korea. However, I couldn't have learned its application to business matters without someone trusting me on this level. It was something that has always stuck with me and has informed many of the decisions I have made as a businessman and as a leader. I have tried to surround myself with quality people and then be willing to trust them to do whatever it is they do well. If you can't trust people, then you shouldn't be working with them. But if you do trust them, let them get to work.

We were off and running with Sail, and I learned so much about running a company during this time. I also learned a lot more about being a father when Cynthia gave birth to our second child on July 1, 1956. This time, we were graced with a beautiful baby girl. We named her Cynthia Ann, but we always just called her Ann.

Within two and a half years, Sam and I had built nine additional gas stations in Tennessee, Kentucky, and Virginia. The company was profitable and, just as he had said he would do, Sam had let me run it completely. His follow through and trust built a sense of confidence in me that I enjoyed not only for myself, but that I also longed to pass down to others. Sam taught me that good leaders cause those who follow them to also want to become good leaders.

I would soon have the chance to lead my own team. In 1958, Sam and his brother worked out a deal to swap interests in the construction company and the oil company. This move would make Sam the principal owner of Fleet, which he planned to combine with Sail to create one new company under the name Fleet. This left me working for the new combined company.

Once again, Sam offered to let me invest in the new company, just as he had done when I took the job at Sail. But this moment felt like a crossroads for me. I wasn't sure I wanted to work for the new combined company. Rather than work for someone else again, I had learned so much about the oil business that I felt more inclined to try to make something happen on my own terms.

Sam had been very good to me, but, from a business and future perspective, he understood where I was coming from. We worked out a deal in which he bought out my stock in Sail Oil, which had grown to about $50,000 in value, so that I could have start-up capital to launch out on my own as an entrepreneur. We also drew up some non-compete language that guaranteed I would not build any gas stations in Tennessee that would compete with Sail over the next five years.

By the fall of 1958, our third child, Bill, was about to be born. It was a season of new things in our family and our business. I already had an idea of what I wanted to call the new company. It was a name that caught my eye from an insurance advertisement I saw while traveling through North Carolina.

On October 1, 1958, our new company was incorporated under the name Pilot Oil Corporation.

Co-pilots

Ready or not, the company was off and running. I'd had some experience running a business like this before, but things are much different when the responsibility is all yours. I was going to need every bit of my previous experience—and much more.

There's so much I could tell about the nuts and bolts of how Pilot came together in the early years, but it's less of a story about facts, figures, and agreements and more a story about people. For our purposes here, I'd like to focus on three people in particular. Without these three partners, there is simply no way we ever would have made it. In fact, I personally couldn't have made it without any single one of them, which once again just proves how lucky I was to have all three.

In business and in life, you need three people to make things run smoothly: a good lawyer, a good accountant/tax person, and a good banker. We measure our success throughout the years by the quality of the people who work with us—and by that rubric, these three people made Pilot very successful.

The first key person to Pilot's success was Bob Campbell—yes, the same Bob Campbell who had crossed Cumberland Avenue on a whim to enter law school. Bob was also one of my Sigma Chi fraternity brothers. His inclination to enter law school proved to be a good one. After he earned his law degree, he came on board to help us incorporate Pilot and get things moving in the right direction. Throughout the course of any business or career, having good legal representation is imperative—and Bob Campbell always represented us with the highest level of excellence.

The thing I admired the most about Bob, as is generally the case with any true professional worth his or her salt, was that he knew what he didn't know. In other words, he didn't try to act as if he were already an expert on every situation we faced. He was most certainly confident, but he didn't let his confidence lead to haughty, careless, or reckless outcomes. He remained humble enough to keep learning at every stage, no matter how big or successful the company became.

I think this is a key component for any strong leader, one that is often lost when one views leadership as purely a matter of influence or skill. The bottom line is that, if you think you know everything, you are just asking for trouble. Bob Campbell was the best example of this kind of humble tenacity to keep searching for solutions that were seemingly beyond his purview without rushing headlong into the unknown with overconfidence. We wouldn't be where we are today without Bob Campbell's expertise. To this day, Bob remains one of my closest lifelong friends.

The second person was the late Jim Shelby, a CPA. His brother, Russell, had worked with me at Fleet Oil and had made a small investment in Sam Claiborne's Sail Oil startup, just like I had done. Jim had also worked at Sail here and there, picking up a little work while he was in school at the University of Tennessee. By the time we started Pilot, Jim had graduated with a degree in accounting and had started working for an accounting firm in Knoxville.

Jim went on to have a very distinguished career in accounting as a partner at Arthur Andersen and a managing partner of Coopers & Lybrand in Knoxville. He also served as the bookkeeper both for Sail and Pilot. When Jim first started with us at Pilot, he worked out of the dining room of our home. That's what I call a *family connection*.

Jim Shelby was a man of complete integrity and high standards who lived by the mantra, *do it the right way*. He understood that financial reporting is the basis for all business. It determines whether banks will lend to you, investors will buy into your company, or suppliers will sell you their products. Everything in a company hinges upon your financial statements, so they better be accurate. Jim was the perfect guy for the job: an upfront and honest friend who was excellent at his craft.

Furthermore, on the personal front, Jim was the person who enabled me to get all my stock distributed to my children, ensuring that my family estate was in good shape for their future. From the right plans to the right figures, Jim made sure everything was audited and accurate.

Jim Shelby passed away in 2012, and he is sorely missed. He literally signed every tax return from Pilot's inception in 1958 up until his death more than fifty years later. His influence, legacy, and friendship all continue to deeply affect me and the entire company today.

The third key person was Jimmy Smith. Jimmy was yet another Sigma Chi from UT, one year my senior. He functioned in a role that could best be described as my "thought partner" in business. He was a banker and also served on Pilot's Board of Directors for a long, long time.

As most startups can attest, when we founded Pilot, we had very little capital to work with, so we had to borrow money all the time. Jimmy helped by pointing us to the banks we should talk to about the right products for what we were trying to accomplish in any specific move.

Jimmy was extremely innovative, seeing clearly the lay of the land ahead of us. He always thought of ways to help the business not only stay on firm financial ground, but also take the necessary next steps to keep moving forward. He stood by us through thick and thin.

I miss Jim Shelby—and Bob Campbell and Jimmy Smith are still my best friends today. It is impossible to separate their story from the history of Pilot. There is no chance we would be where we are without them.

First Steps

Since I had agreed with Sam Claiborne that we wouldn't build any locations close to his gas stations for the first five years, we found ourselves working mainly outside our own backyard in Knoxville, even though it was our corporate home base. With all of the location work I had done with Fleet and Sail, I was intimately familiar with the Virginia and Kentucky areas. In October 1958, we bought a piece of property in Roanoke where we could build our first Pilot gas station. But, as it turned out, our first gallon of Pilot gas would not be sold from our first Pilot gas station.

I began regularly driving back and forth between Knoxville and Roanoke, working on getting the gas station built and scouting other possible locations. On one of these trips, as I was about to cross the Virginia–Tennessee state line, I stopped off to see an old friend in the town of Gate City, Virginia.

Just as it still is today, the gasoline and cigarette taxes were higher in Tennessee than they were in Virginia. This differentiation spawned the proliferation of cut-rate gas stations where these products could be bought at a lower price by people who lived near the state line. Gate City was only about five miles from the line.

My friend Vernon Bays owned one of these gas stations. Vernon had been one of our wholesale customers when I worked at Fleet, and I stopped by just because I was just curious how things were going in his neck of the woods. When I pulled up to his location, I was shocked to discover that he actually wasn't selling gas. When I asked him about it, he said he had had some financial woes with the business that were preventing him from selling fuel, so he was just selling cigarettes.

It was obvious that he no longer wanted to be in this business, so I said, "Vernon, why don't you sell me this gas station?"

He looked at me with curiosity, intrigued by the prospect.

"How much do you want for it?" I inquired.

He thought for a few seconds, then said, "$10,000."

That was outside of my budget, so I said, "Well, I can give you $6,000."

"Can you close on Monday?"

This was Thursday, mind you, but I said, "Yes, we can make that happen."

Vernon agreed. On the next Monday, November 20, 1958, we paid him $6,000 and Gate City instantly became the first Pilot station to actually become operational—and that afternoon, we sold our first gallon of Pilot gasoline from what would officially be our second location.

In those days, customers often used cash tickets that had to be stamped so they would have an official document to reference with their expense account records. This meant each gas station had to have its own unique location number—a number that would often be used for customers' cash tickets. We assigned the number 102 to the Gate City location. One might think that it would have made more sense just to use the number one, but we had done the same thing at Sail. We didn't want to start off with the number one because it would make our company and its locations seem like a pretty small operation (even though it *was*). So we started with 102 for Gate City, while the location still being built in Roanoke was 101.

We certainly were off and running, but we were already running short on capital. We had used up the money from the sale of Sail and technically, we had only one gas station open at the time, which was in Gate City. The store in Roanoke finally opened up in early spring of 1959, which helped increase the stream of revenue, but even while we waited for new stores to be built, we remained focused on adding new locations. Once again, this was a strategy that could not have been accomplished without the tireless work and expertise of our team, including Bob, Jim, and Jimmy.

Right before Christmas of 1958, we acquired another piece of property in Galax, Virginia, which is a little town close to the North Carolina state line. Our goal in those days was to find locations where there wasn't a lot of independent competition in the area. Galax fit the bill perfectly, as there were no other independent gas stations anywhere near it. This became our third store, positioned somewhat on the way between Gate City and Roanoke, which was a good fit both strategically and logistically.

We also continued to expand into Kentucky, which had always proved to be a good market when I worked for Fleet and Sail. Most of Sam Claiborne's stations were located off US Route 25, which still runs through what is now Interstate 75. Most of his Kentucky stations were in the southeastern region of the commonwealth, so we went up to Prestonsburg, which is farther northeast on the Big Sandy River. This became our fourth location, followed by locations in Danville and in Louisville. Within the first five years of Pilot, we were blessed to have opened six locations.

Our strategy for opening new locations was multifaceted. For some, we simply leased the properties upfront with the intention of purchasing them later after more capital was generated from their respective sales. For others, we implemented a hybrid strategy. Using raw numbers as an example, if a property cost $25,000, we would try to get the seller to let us buy it for $5,000 to $10,000 down with the intent of the seller financing the remaining balance over ten years. And, of course, we built some new locations from scratch, which cost between $20,000 to $25,000. Thus, our total investment to have a store up and running was around $45,000 to $50,000. However, we would only invest about $20,000 directly out of pocket in the project, with the intent of borrowing the rest from a local bank. The strategy worked effectively, affording us enough capital to keep expanding while also ensuring that each location was somewhat standing on its own two feet in under ten years.

This was our plan and it seemed to be working well for the first several years of our young company. However, nothing ever works out

> On the next Monday, November 20, 1958, we paid him $6,000 and Gate City instantly became the first Pilot station to actually become operational—and that afternoon, we sold our first gallon of Pilot gasoline from what would officially be our second location.

completely according to plan—not in real life, anyway. We were off and running for sure, but life always has a way of making the journey more interesting than you expect it to be.

CHAPTER 5

CONVENIENCE AND TRAGEDY

Putting on More Steam

WHEN I LOOK BACK AT THIS SEASON OF OUR LIFE AND THE EARLY growth of Pilot, it is easy to focus solely on the good things that happened. Being an optimist at heart makes this doubly easy. However, I don't want you to read this book and only hear about healthy growth statistics that happened over the course of multiple years as if nothing negative happened during all that time—because it most certainly did. Pilot was about to grow even more, but this did not mean we had no bumps in the road along the way.

These bumps helped make us who we are today.

To that end, General Neyland's third game maxim speaks directly to the posture we attempted to take during this season. *If at first the game—or a break—goes against you, don't slow down or get rattled. Put on more steam.* I truly think this is the main difference between winning and losing in all aspects of life. You cannot control the cards you are dealt from your birth; that is, you can't choose what family you are born to, what your nationality or ethnicity will be, or whether you are raised under horrible or wonderful conditions. All people do not start on equal footing—this is one of the reasons I feel both lucky and gladly obligated to give back. Even though all people don't start at an equal position, all people are created by God to have equal value.

I believe General Neyland was right when he taught us that, when things don't go our way, we should "put on more steam"; that is, we should not give up but press ahead with more vigor and boldness, no matter what situation we find ourselves in. And yes, sometimes we will have people around us who simply don't have the means, strength, or circumstantial ability to put on more steam, which means we have to serve them well by pushing ahead on their behalf.

> If at first the game—or a break—goes against you, don't slow down or get rattled. Put on more steam.

We shouldn't do this recklessly or foolishly, but we certainly shouldn't allow difficulty to convince us that present circumstances are the way things will always be. If everyone stopped at his or her biggest speed bump in life, then no one would ever make it further down any road—and no one would help anyone else make it down their own roads either. We all have speed bumps; to get over them, you have to push the gas at least a little bit either for yourself or for those around you. Or, as the General would say it, you have to *put on more steam*.

I guess you could say we were literally "pushing the gas" during the late 1950s and early 1960s. We had six locations, and our financial strategy for getting them up and running for the short term was somewhat working. However, we were certainly limited in our ability to expand the business at the rate we desired.

After the five-year term of our non-compete agreement with Sam Claiborne had expired, we began expanding more into the Tennessee and southern Kentucky areas. We opened our first Knoxville location on Cumberland Avenue in the heart of the University of Tennessee campus. It was an existing location on which the lease had run out. Our seventh location—and our first in Tennessee—was born.

After this, we opened another location in Roanoke, as well as others in Blacksburg, Pearisburg, and Stanton. All told, we were having pretty good success in the Virginia area. We then opened stores in London, Kentucky; Covington, Virginia; and then another one in Knoxville on Kingston Pike. This was where our office was located for many years.

But again, the breaks didn't always go our way, even though we were moving the ball down the field. Our location in Prestonsburg proved to be a failure. I guess there was a good reason why few gas stations had been opened there. It was a difficult decision because you always want to see yourself moving forward, but it just wasn't going to work. So we punted and closed the store, cutting our losses. We just couldn't afford to keep a station open that wasn't yielding a consistent profit, especially as we were trying to continually expand the company into other locations.

Our margin was paper thin—and this store just didn't make the cut.

Marathon

It may seem as if we were sprinting ahead with Pilot, but these first six or seven years were most definitely filled with their fair share of challenges. Even though we were excited and seemingly making progress, there was a moment when we hit the wall. After we had built twelve locations in Virginia, Kentucky, and Tennessee, we found ourselves extremely leveraged as we waited on long-term returns on our investments. This caused us to become financially limited to opening more stores. We *wanted* to build more, but we simply couldn't.

This wasn't just a desire to expand. Jim Shelby told me we had to build more locations in order to sustain the amount of overhead we had acquired. So then, expansion was not only *desirable*, but also *necessary* for sustaining what we had built up to that point. Jim's concern was valid, but where were we going to get the money?

As I said, the people I trust have always pushed us ahead, especially when we have stalled. In this case, I reached out to my old buddy Jimmy Smith about our situation. Creative as always, he went to work on an "outside the box" solution that would surpass what we had done up to that point to acquire operational and expansive capital.

The answer came in the form of Marathon Oil, the country's largest supplier of independents like us. At the end of 1964 and after months of discussion, they made an offer buy 50 percent of Pilot, something I really didn't want to do at the time. However, the deal came with the stipulation that they would also loan us $2 million we could use to continue opening more stores.

> The answer came in the form of Marathon Oil, the country's largest supplier of independents like us.

At this time, opening a new location cost us about $50,000, so we did the math and quickly figured out that taking this deal would enable us to build *forty* more stores. This was huge! We only had twelve stores at the time, so adding forty more would be a 400 percent increase in property and revenue—and that's pretty darn good. They also told us when this initial loan ran out, they would loan us another $2 million as long as everything was on track and going well.

Even though the numbers looked promising, this was an extremely difficult decision. After all, when you have started a business from the ground up, you feel a sense of responsibility to keep its assets and future outlook somewhat accessible so you can guard them with the same diligence you used to get them started in the first place. Their proposal was a big risk, but it was also a big opportunity.

Since hindsight is 20/20, we can look back at this metaphorical mile of our company's "marathon" and wholeheartedly say that this was a very good decision, so much so that we call it our *fifth break*.

On October 1, 1965, we sold half the company to Marathon. Suddenly, we had the financial room to breathe that we so desperately needed, getting us over the speed bump. This deal allowed us to expand in the way we really dreamed we could do, so much so that, by 1975, we had grown to over seventy-six gas stations. Our 400 percent projection ended up being more like 600 percent!

Marathon's interest in our growth fueled the partnership, but their oversight was minimal. All they wanted to do was approve any new locations we proposed, something they were generally eager to do because it increased business for both of us.

This was a pivotal moment in our company's history. The partnership with Marathon was yet another thing I could have never produced on my own. We knew that we needed a break, but there was no way to manufacture this opportunity. I'm not surprised it came through the work of people I trust, like Jimmy Smith. When the break did come, we did our best to make the most of it—just like General Neyland taught me.

Rethinking Stores

During this time, we mainly sold only gasoline and cigarettes. This was the operational reality of most gas stations at the time. We also sold soft drinks and Lance® cookies, but again, gas and cigarettes were our chief commodities—and the main things that customers had always expected from a gas station.

As interstate travel continued to expand, some gas stations began to sell some other items. We took notice of the trend and took a creative look at our own company. We had a lot of money wrapped up in the properties, so the question of whether to sell more items to increase revenue and accommodate our customers' changing expectations was a valid one, to say the least. We began wondering if we were leaving quite a bit of money on the table.

Other gas stations had begun converting their existing locations into what they called convenience stores. After much consideration, this seemed to be a wise move for us as well. At the start of the convenience store trend, the main difference between our existing gas stations and convenience stores was the sale of beer. As I will discuss later, I have never been a beer drinker—in fact, I have never drunk alcohol of any kind—so some of this was foreign to me. Regardless, we began to explore whether to sell beer in our Pilot stores.

A funny conversation during this time really drove home the point that people were expecting gas stations to offer more than just gas and cigarettes. We had just built a store in Anniston, Alabama, which was about fifty miles from Birmingham. I was going back and forth regularly to check on the construction with the contractors and crew. One day, I asked one of the carpenters how long it would take me to get back to Birmingham from there.

"You're about two beers away," he said.

We had a good laugh, but ironically enough, Anniston, Alabama, was the first store to "pilot" the sale of beer. From that point forward, we were fully into the convenience store business—and it was a very important move for us. If we had not adapted to the changing cultural landscape, we would have been left behind. Little did we know how much more society would change in the years to come, but this was a crucial first step for us in reimagining what a "gas station" could really be. This also was important to understanding the way we would build new gas stations in the future, or in some cases, acquire other stations to convert into Pilot convenience stores.

To that end, there was a man named Bill Lonas in Knoxville who owned a company called Lonas Oil. Bill had been in the gasoline business all his life, working for a company called Dixie Vim before founding Lonas Oil Company. By 1978, he owned about twenty gas stations in East Tennessee. We had become friends during the time I worked for Sam Claiborne, as Bill had been one of our wholesale customers.

We had stayed in contact over the years and, after much conversation and negotiation, we worked out a deal to buy his twenty stores—and his entire company—for about $3 million. It was a good deal and, since his company had a good amount of working capital, we were able to finance the acquisition. This purchase was significant because it propelled us deeper into the convenience store business, especially in terms of market share in the Knoxville area. I honestly don't think we could have had as much success in this part of our business without this purchase. By the time we fully closed the deal, we had about eighteen locations in Knoxville.

This gave us a critical mass of locations that would enable us to fully enter into the convenience store business. Our first project involved tearing down our gas station on Alcoa Highway to convert the location into a full-scale convenience store.

My oldest son, Jimmy Haslam, had just started working for us full-time during this same year. One of his first tasks was to get this location converted into a convenience store. He asked me how to do it; of course, I had no idea.

From that point forward, we were fully into the convenience store business—and it was a very important move for us.

But I did know some people who had done it, so I gave their information to Jimmy and told him to figure it out himself—which he did. He completely exceeded all expectations and took our company to places it had never been before. It was at this point that I first realized what a great leader Jimmy was and would continue to be in the years to come.

Beginning with the Marathon deal in 1965 and followed by the Lonas deal in 1976, the years to come brought about a mass expansion and conversion effort into this new paradigm. By 1980, when my other son Bill joined the company, we had around one hundred and twenty gas station convenience stores.

The face of Pilot had truly changed.

When Tragedy Strikes

There is one event in particular that occurred during this season between 1965 and 1980 that stands out above all the rest. It was one of the defining and tragic moments of our life—certainly not one that I would have ever expected.

On December 5, 1974, I was in Washington, D.C., for a Sigma trade association meeting. The meetings had ended earlier than expected, so I took a commercial flight to Asheville and then a private plane brought me back to a small regional airport called Island Home in Knoxville. I had a car phone, which was not very common in those days, so I made a call home to let Cynthia know that I was coming home early. My daughter, Ann, answered the phone and I could tell that something was terribly wrong. She just said, "Daddy, come home quick."

> **With broken hearts, they informed me that Cynthia had passed away.**

When I arrived at the house, there were cars everywhere. Before I could make it up the front steps, Jimmy, Ann, and Bill came out of the house to meet me. I could tell by the look on their faces that something terrible had happened. With broken hearts, they informed me that Cynthia had passed away.

It's hard to describe the depth of this loss in our family. Cynthia was only forty-two years old, and I was only a year older. Bill, our youngest, was still a junior in high school. Ann was a freshman at UT. Jimmy was a junior at UT, working for Pilot part-time while he finished up college. We were all so young, all things considering. It just didn't seem possible.

Ann and Bill still lived at home, and Jimmy lived in a little house on the property. That morning, Cynthia had made everyone's breakfast and then went back to bed. Later that day, when Ann came home from school, she couldn't get her to wake up. Ann called for help, but it was soon apparent that her mother had already died.

As it turned out, Cynthia had died from a ruptured aorta caused by congenital heart condition she inherited from her father. He died at the age of thirty under similar circumstances. Some years later, Ann had several heart operations to address the same issue. But for Cynthia at that point in time, the technology or knowledge didn't exist to address and correct her condition. In the present under different circumstances, she might have survived.

We were surrounded by friends that day, something for which I will always be thankful. Cynthia's best friend, Natalie, was one of the first ones to arrive at the house, as was our priest and long-time friend, Dan Matthews. Needless to say, it was a traumatic event at a formative moment. Our kids were almost all grown. Our business was growing and thriving. Despite all these positives, one major negative from one single moment left me facing life as a single dad of three at the age of forty-three.

New Seasons

After Cynthia's funeral and all the difficulties of going through the aftermath around the holidays, we began figuring out our next steps to move forward, even while we were grieving. Life was difficult during this time, as would be expected. I am grateful that our children were old enough to process the loss with some maturity, but, in many ways, losing a mother at such critical moments in their lives made each passing milestone all the more difficult. Graduations. New romances. New jobs. Weddings. There was so much life happening all around us, which was a blessing because it kept us in motion; but it also reminded us that one of us was no longer there to share in the experiences. It was so hard, but we kept going the best we could, knowing that God was with us and that this was what Cynthia would have wanted us to do.

Cynthia had been a member of Pilot's board since its inception, so we needed to replace her position. The board voted to replace her with our son Jimmy, who was only twenty years old at the time. The next year, after he graduated from college, Jimmy officially came on board to work at Pilot. He had worked in our stores throughout high school and college, so he knew the lay of the land, and I knew he was ready to take on more responsibility. As the years passed, my intuition about him would be correct. He became the CEO in 1996 and has been responsible for the tremendous growth of Pilot Company for the past twenty-five years.

> During those dark moments, I had no way of knowing that I would marry an incredible woman who has remained by my side for forty-four years and counting.

Again, Bill Haslam came on board at Pilot in 1980. All my children turned out to be creative, dependable, and successful in their own unique ways. Working with them in business and in philanthropy has been yet another one of God's many blessings.

Other things began to change in our family as well. After Cynthia passed away, I married one of her closest friends, Natalie Leach Tucker, about a year and a half later. She had been a personal friend to our entire family since our days at the University of Tennessee. When I lost Cynthia, there were times when the path forward for my life was difficult to see—at times, all hope seemed lost. During those dark moments, I had no way of knowing that I would marry an incredible woman who has remained by my side for forty-four years and counting. Besides that, I also gained three beautiful daughters, Jennie, Susan, and Carol, whom I love with all my heart, along with their wonderful families.

Life was hard during this season, but God was completely faithful.

CHAPTER 6

NEW DIRECTIONS

The Silliest Thing

By 1980, we had over a hundred convenience stores, the company was making money, the relationship with Marathon was going well, and things were moving in the right direction all around. But, as luck would have it, everything was about to take a turn that we never could have predicted—and it all started with something I never believed could work.

One day, a salesman for Marathon, Burl Martin, called us and asked if we knew Kenny Pritchard. I did indeed know him; he was an Amoco jobber in Jackson, Mississippi. Burl went on to tell us that Kenny had opened a convenience store in Slidell, Louisiana, on I-10 . . . but with a twist: he had put six diesel pumps on the backside of the building.

My first reaction said it all, "That's the silliest thing I've ever heard!"

Back then, it seemed absurd to mix the two worlds of commercial trucking and noncommercial interstate travel. Even so, Burl's comments intrigued us enough to take a trip down to Slidell to talk to Kenny in person and see what he was doing.

On January 3, 1981, Jimmy and I flew down see him. I vividly remember that the airport was surrounded by pine trees. It felt as if we had literally landed smack dab in the sticks. And we live in East

Tennessee, so that's saying something. I told Jimmy this was going to be a waste of our time.

We were already there, though, and since Kenny had been gracious enough to meet with us, we stayed the course and went to his store. The University of Alabama had just played in the Sugar Bowl in New Orleans, so there were a lot of people traveling back to Alabama from southern Louisiana. We pulled up to see all kinds of cars buying gas, but, to our surprise, there were also a lot of tractor trailers buying diesel fuel on the other side of the store.

Suddenly this began to look like something we should pay attention to.

Kenny was incredibly kind, sharing everything with us about his operation. It was the first time we had ever seen a gas station work in this manner, so we had a lot of questions. Before we left, we literally paced off the area to get rough dimensions so we could possibly integrate something like this in our Pilot stores.

When we came back home, Jimmy and I spent several months mulling over the idea. He was more excited about it than I was, but we finally decided to try it at a single location to see what the results might be. The next step was figuring out where to build such a store, so we reached out to a former employee named Jack Meade, who was then doing location work for McDonald's. We told him we were looking for a possible location in Kentucky, because the diesel taxes were lower there than they were in Tennessee. However, we didn't want it to be too far north in Kentucky since it would be a new, experimental operation. We wanted to be able to get there pretty quickly to check on things.

Jack told us about a location south of Cincinnati on I-75, so Jimmy and I decided to fly up to check it out. Before we went, Jack suggested another property just north of Lexington. We still wanted something closer, so, while we were flying up there, I was poring over an atlas searching for possibilities.

"What about Corbin, Kentucky?" I asked. I knew that the small town of Corbin would be closer to Knoxville and sure enough, Jack said he knew of a piece of property there that might work. So we told our pilot to land the plane in Corbin—and it turned out to be just what we were looking for.

In November of 1981, we opened our first travel center in Corbin, Kentucky. Once again, luck played such a big factor because, if we hadn't gone down to Slidell on the advice of Burl Martin, and if Kenny Prichard hadn't been kind enough to share the concept with us, and if we hadn't known Jack, who happened to be familiar with the real estate in the area, and if Corbin hadn't been a good location...well, let's just say that's a lot of *ifs* that worked out in our favor, so much so that I consider the opening of this first travel center in Corbin to be the beginning of our *sixth break*. It was the first installment of many new changes in direction for the company.

> In November of 1981, we opened our first travel center in Corbin, Kentucky.

The Corbin location was important because when you are attempting to build a chain of any kind of business, the first location can make or break you. In this case, it was a huge success, and we quickly learned that travel centers seemed to generate exponentially greater profit than gas stations or even convenience stores. Thus we began to shift our focus from convenience stores to travel centers.

West of the Mississippi

By the 1980s, travel centers were beginning to catch on. The nation was becoming much more mobile, both commercially and with families utilizing the newly completed interstate highway system to take more trips across the country.

We were lucky to be entering the travel center business just as demand was beginning to rise. From 1981 to 1987, we built about twenty Pilot Travel Centers. Our first experience in Corbin proved not to be a fluke: our new travel centers were much more profitable than our convenience stores. We knew it was time to fully embrace the idea of expanding our travel center network, but there were going to be some hurdles we had to cross to get there.

The first hurdle had to do with the way we had always done business with our partner, Marathon. Things had been great with them, and it had proven to be a mutually advantageous relationship for many years. We were buying their products, paying them dividends, and, despite a few of the expected bumps that any business relationship experiences, everything had remained very satisfactory with them.

But by the end of 1987, we began talking to Marathon about our desire to build a nationwide chain of travel centers. At the time, Marathon only had products available east of the Mississippi, so they really weren't keen on the idea of Pilot's expansion west of the Mississippi into markets where they would no longer be our sole supplier. In fact, there was a bit of friction with them when we opened a travel center in Kingman, Arizona.

However, we were intent on building a nationwide chain, so we kept talking and negotiating with them. Frankly, the talks were going nowhere fast. Marathon's Vice-President of marketing was a man named Corky Frank. Corky was a Texas A&M graduate and an accomplished businessman. He was smart and savvy, and we liked him a lot, but we just couldn't seem to make headway with him on our attempts to expand the business westward or purchase Marathon's interest in Pilot.

Another good friend of ours, Dick White, Marathon's wholesale manager, suggested that I change the venue a bit to help make a better connection with Corky. It was common knowledge that Corky loved good food and desserts, so we invited him to go with us to Blackberry Farm, a picturesque resort near the foothills of the Smoky Mountains just south of Knoxville in Walland, Tennessee. He accepted our invitation.

That was the trip when I discovered the hidden secret to advancing a tense and tedious business negotiation: a good crème brûlée. As it turned out, Corky loved the stuff, so I had the waiter keep 'em coming. I guess it *sweetened the deal* just enough, because we were able to hammer out the basic parameters of a deal to change our relationship with Marathon.

Once we had this general concept in place and Corky had taken it back to his people at Marathon, they brought a team of executives back to Knoxville to resolve the nitty gritty details of the deal. The basic plan was that they would retain a third of the locations, along with a cash buyout from us, and we would keep the remaining two-thirds of the locations. The sticky part was that we had to come to some consensus about which locations would be theirs and which would be ours.

We had done a lot of our own internal research regarding what we wanted out of these locations, and, of course, they had done the same. Our friend Dick White and a host of other Marathon representatives came to our house on Lyons Bend Road on a Saturday to meet with Jimmy, Bill, and me to try to put the whole thing to bed. Most of the day entailed going back and forth on details. When we would make a proposition, they would go out on our back porch and deliberate for about thirty minutes before coming back with their counterproposal.

However, when we would step away to the front porch to consider their counterproposal, it would generally only take us about five minutes before we returned with an answer. This back and forth continued all afternoon, each time our "back" being significantly shorter than their "forth." When they finally brought us what seemed to be their final offer, I told Jimmy and Bill that we should wait on our front porch for about thirty minutes this time—and we did. It worked.

On June 30, 1988, we ended up with two-thirds of the company, which positioned us to really pursue the process of building a nation-wide chain of travel centers. Again, all of this made up our *sixth break*: our successful movement forward into the travel center business.

Family and Partners

As a leader, I never wanted to be found holding on to power so long that I missed significant opportunities to pass along the torch to other capable leaders around me while I could still support them. Don't get me wrong; I have never desired to stop working. At the time of this writing, I am eighty-nine years old and, much to Natalie's distress, I am still just like all our Pilot stores: open twenty-four hours a day, three hundred and sixty-five days a year.

Even so, I have always known that this business is not all about me. And if I were ever to allow it to be all about me, I would only succeed in making myself the ceiling of our success. I have always known that if I want the company to grow beyond what I can make it, I must share leadership with other trusted leaders.

> I think it is a mistake to wait for life's circumstances to determine when a crucial moment of power sharing or transition should occur.

Imagine my joy when these trusted leaders turned out to be my own children. As Pilot continued to grow, it became apparent that Jimmy and Bill needed to have more of the reins of the company moving forward—and that they didn't need to wait until I couldn't do it anymore. They needed to start leading now.

I think it is a mistake to wait for life's circumstances to determine when a crucial moment of power sharing or transition should occur. If leaders don't begin sharing the weights and wins of the business while they are still around to guide, support, and help along the way, then, at the very least, they are delaying their successors' development. Instead of being able to learn from decisions—and, yes, mistakes—while the founding leader is still around to help shoulder the load, they are forced to stand alone under the bright, hot lights of leadership. I didn't want to do this to those who would someday lead the company in my place. I wanted to lead *with* them as soon as possible.

When it became apparent that Jimmy and Bill wanted to continue with the company for the long-term, I knew it was time to discuss what the future (and present) might hold for us as a team. Jimmy was already heading up most of our operations work, while Bill was doing a lot of the administrative and location work.

I sat them down and told them my plan: when I turned sixty-five, one of them would become President and one of them would become CEO. They agreed and, on January 1, 1996, Jimmy became the CEO and Bill became the President of Pilot. I retained the position of Chairman of the Board.

This was such a fun time in our lives and, believe it or not, we worked really well together. This is not to say that we always agreed on everything, but in business, the goal is not always to completely agree but, rather to listen to one another and make the big picture better than it would have been if only one person's opinion had been expressed.

I don't have to wait or wonder if Pilot is going to be in good hands *someday*. I have been able to witness Pilot resting in good hands *today*.

To that end, the values of family are interwoven into every unique thread of the history and growth of our company. In fact, you can't separate the Pilot Company from the Haslam family—the two have always gone hand in hand. I am so proud that five Haslam family members have held significant roles in leadership in the company at some point in time, each adding their own unique contributions to our advancement and enrichment.

By the turn of the century, we had built a fairly large chain of travel centers and things were seemingly running well with our leadership, operations, and processes. However, we found we were creeping back into debt because it cost so much more money to build travel centers. Back in the mid-1990s, we had entered into a partnership with the Louis Dreyfus Company, a commodity-trading firm. This enabled us to build ten more locations before we bought them out.

That experience got us thinking about whether or not we should pursue another investment partner. Morgan Stanley helped us look for prospective partners and, after a lot of research on their end, we couldn't believe who they brought to the table: Marathon.

Lo and behold, we entered into another partnership with Marathon, which by that time had built or acquired a chain of over one hundred Speedway Travel Centers. Pilot had nearly two hundred travel centers at this point. We ended up setting up another fifty-fifty deal with them, which gave us a chain of nearly three hundred and fifty travel centers. Then, in 2003, we bought the Williams Travel Centers chain of forty-two stores. Things were going well, and we were growing by both building new stores and acquiring others. It was a winning formula.

In time, though, Marathon entered into a state of change and reorganization that resulted in us buying them out again in 2008. This time, we were able to bring in a private-equity company, CVC, as our new investment partner. Once again, we owned just over 50 percent of the company—a company that now operated approximately four hundred travel centers nationwide.

Flying Leaps

Our next break was truly transformational. When we became deeply involved in the travel center business, there were three big companies that made up most of the market. We (Pilot) were the largest, Flying J was the next largest, and Truck Stops of America was the third. Truck Stops of America had been in business longer than any of us, boasting the largest truck stops and travel centers in terms of facilities. We had the smallest facilities, while Flying J's facilities were somewhere in between.

The recession of 2008 hit all our companies. However, it seemed to negatively affect Flying J the worst. This was because Flying J wasn't just in the travel center business; they were also in both the pipeline and the refining industries. When things took a downward turn, they simply couldn't recover on their own and eventually had to file for Chapter 11 bankruptcy in December 2008.

Flying J was founded by Jay Call. Tragically, Jay had died in an airplane crash a few years earlier and the management of the company had made some mistakes that resulted in this bankruptcy. Jay's daughter, Crystal Maggalot, then took over as the CEO and was working hard to pick up the pieces.

This led to our *seventh break.*

Jimmy began speaking with Crystal in March 2009 about the idea of Pilot taking over Flying J. After constant contact between the two of them, we signed an agreement in July to combine our two companies and pay them the money they needed to get out of bankruptcy. Flying J would retain a certain percentage of the stock in our company, but we would own the majority.

I cannot overstate how complicated this deal was, so much so that it took over a year to finalize. After working it out with Flying J, we next had to secure the financing from the banks. However, the biggest hurdle was securing the approval of the Federal Trade Commission. A year is a long time to work on details, but Jimmy never gave up.

When the dust settled, our new company, Pilot Flying J (later referred to simply as Pilot Company), now had nearly six hundred travel centers nationwide.

The deal was finally approved on June 30, 2010. We took over Flying J on July 1. I don't believe anyone one else but Jimmy could have worked this deal out, especially through such an arduous process. Once again, his dogged determination as a leader changed the course of our company.

When the dust settled, our new company, Pilot Flying J (later referred to simply as Pilot Company), now had nearly six hundred travel centers nationwide. This combining of our companies changed so many things about Pilot for the better. Flying J had huge truck stops. Their locations featured more parking spaces than ours. Their stores also had drivers' lounges and other amenities that made them much more driver friendly from a facilities perspective. Each one even boasted a full-service restaurant that seated about one hundred people, which we converted to Denny's restaurants. Some of them even had barbershops. Their facilities helped elevate our company so we could offer so much more than what we were ever able to offer before.

This deal also included an investment interest from CVC Capital, which we later bought out, leaving us with over 75 percent ownership. This big break—the Flying J deal—pushed us further ahead in the travel center business than we could have ever imagined. It remains a monumental part of our story. The most significant improvement to the company came through the expanded geographical coverage we gained with the addition of their stores. Pilot stores were mainly located in the Southeast and Midwest during that time, with few stores west of the Mississippi River. Flying J stores, on the other hand, were concentrated in the Rockies and on the West Coast. With this one move, Pilot stores almost instantaneously gained nationwide coverage. This was a true game-changer for our company.

Jimmy Haslam is more than just some fortunate son who inherited a leadership role in a company. As a former CEO myself who still constantly evaluates executives and their leadership effectiveness, I can truthfully say that Jimmy Haslam is nothing less than a phenomenal leader in his own right.

Not just with the Flying J deal, but through every major change of our company including the Lonas deal in the late 1970s, multiple agreements with Marathon, and the Berkshire Hathaway partnership I am about to describe, he has shown persistence and determination, even when he was navigating some of these high-stakes situations at a young age in life. He is a natural learner with a high degree of intellectual curiosity, a great operator with high standards and propensity for numbers, and a high-level networker who always leads by example and makes sure he is the hardest worker in the room.

I was twenty-seven years old when we started Pilot. Jimmy was only twenty-one when he came on board. We both started at this company when we were young and we both have worked here all our lives. This is a legacy that brings me so much joy every day. The fact is, Jimmy and I have always worked really well together. It has been a lot of fun to see so many incredible leadership attributes emerge and develop in my own son. To say I'm proud would not begin to describe my feelings for his character and leadership.

Partnerships for the Future

The *eighth break* came out of nowhere in much the same way. In 2017, Byron Trott, the founder of an investment banking firm in Chicago, BDT Capital Partners, owned a small interest (about 4.5 percent) in Pilot. He had done quite a bit of work with Berkshire Hathaway and was close friends with Warren Buffet. Byron began telling us that Mr. Buffet wanted to take an interest in Pilot.

At first, we were not interested at all, but Byron continued to talk to both parties and eventually brought us some figures that caught our interest. To help ease our worries, they reminded us that nearly fifteen years earlier, Berkshire Hathaway had bought Clayton Homes, one of the largest manufacturers of mobile and modular homes in the nation. Jim Clayton, who is about my age, originally founded the Knoxville-based company, and Berkshire Hathaway bought it after it went public. Jim's son, Kevin, had been running the company since that time. Berkshire Hathaway encouraged us to speak with Kevin Clayton about their relationship with the company.

After speaking with Kevin one day, we were quickly convinced that this partnership could turn out to be one of the best things to ever happen to Pilot. Kevin had assured us that Berkshire Hathaway remained completely hands-off and that they would not interfere with the goals or operations of the business. They just wanted to partner as investors who would help move the company forward.

This deal would indeed become *big break number eight* for us.

In terms of the history of the company, this is a full-circle moment back to the beginning of this book. I've already written about our unlikely meeting with Warren Buffett that ended with a Coke in the corner of the little café in Omaha. But what you don't know is all the other fascinating interactions I've had with Warren.

Warren agreed to come meet with some of our leaders at our general managers' meeting in Orlando, Florida, in 2018. At one point during the day, we had a little private meeting with our senior leadership. Later that evening, we hosted a panel discussion between Warren, Jimmy, and me. Warren did a fantastic job of speaking to our leadership.

After the day's events had concluded, Warren was about to head back to the airport to fly home. I was remaining in Orlando, but Natalie was flying back to Knoxville. Warren had invited Natalie just to catch a ride with him and his assistants back to the airport. It was only supposed to be only about a ten- or fifteen-minute ride…until they encountered a traffic jam resulting from an accident on the interstate.

> When it came to the Berkshire Hathaway deal, I really felt that we could look everyone in the eye and tell them beyond a shadow of a doubt that this was a good deal for everyone at Pilot Company.

An hour later, Natalie was still in the car talking with Warren. We laughed so hard because an hour with Warren Buffett is an item sometimes promoted at charity events. It is not uncommon for one of these hours to be auctioned off for $4 million or $5 million. Natalie, however, got her hour for free, so I guess some of my luck must have rubbed off on her! Truth be told, though, Warren was the *really* lucky one. He got to spend an hour with my Natalie.

The Berkshire Hathaway deal was something that some of our Pilot Company team members initially had a hard time understanding. I think such a move seems scary to those who hope we continue as we always have, especially when it comes to employing team members. Quite frankly, as a private company, Pilot had reached a size where maintaining our function was difficult without taking on a larger, more substantial partner. We knew it had to be the *right* partner, which is why we took our time and endeavored never to make big decisions haphazardly.

Our Pilot Company headquarters is located at the top of a little hill that overlooks I-40 in Knoxville. Everyone who comes either to work or to a meeting at our offices has to drive up that little hill. Driving up that hill is a part of my daily routine and has been for many years. It reminds me that we're always climbing, always working towards leaving the company—and the world—better than we found it. I never make that drive lightly.

I've always told my family that I never want to drive up that hill, come into our offices, and not be able look everyone I see squarely in the eye. When it came to the Berkshire Hathaway deal, I really felt that we could look everyone in the eye and tell them beyond a shadow of a doubt that this was a good deal for everyone at Pilot Company.

The deal is roughly as follows: Berkshire Hathaway bought 38.5 percent of the company, which included portions from Flying J and portions from us. This left us with 50.5 percent of the company, while Flying J retained 11 percent. This is the way the deal was structured for the first five years or so. However, in 2023, Berkshire's interest will increase to 80 percent.

This approaching future reality has been difficult for some people to grasp—and I've even heard some people say that this was a better deal for our *family* than the company. Well, it certainly is good for our family, but I maintain that it is just as good for everyone else as well.

If I were a team member at Pilot, I would want to know a couple of things about the company. The first question would be: are we financially strong? No one wants to drive up the hill one day to find the doors chained and the company in bankruptcy. To answer this question, we made this deal with Berkshire Hathaway because it is the strongest financial company in the world. Our goal was to ensure that Pilot stays strong financially, so this was the best move to ensure such an outcome.

The second thing I would want to know is: who owns the company? This is where perception can be deceptive because, yes, some day Berkshire Hathaway will own 80 percent of the company and Pilot will own 20 percent. Our deal with Berkshire Hathaway guarantees complete ongoing autonomy regarding the ways we operate the company, a company that is guaranteed to remain headquartered right here in the city that has meant so much to our family and our team members over the years.

Because Berkshire Hathaway is our partner, we obviously have to keep sharing financial information with them. However, Pilot Company will not change one bit in terms of its structure and culture. We have tried to create a culture in which team members and guests are valued more highly than profits—and this is a value system Berkshire Hathaway has embraced.

Though I will expound upon them in greater detail in a future chapter, our values state that we will:

+ Value people.
+ Take care of customers.
+ Work hard together.
+ Expect results.

And since they have agreed to allow us to continue running our company according to these values, we are confident that, by God's grace, good results will continue.

The bottom line is that the kind of deal we have with Berkshire Hathaway is one I don't think we could have accomplished with any other company. It reflects a high degree of mutual understanding and agreed autonomy. I truly believe that long after I'm gone, Pilot Company team members will still be driving up that hill to work for a company that is financially secure, continues to value people above profits, and works hard to serve its teams members and customers.

This is where we are today. Obviously, there is no way I can communicate every important detail along the way. There are thousands of stories and thousands of seemingly inconsequential events that have merged together to form this incredible narrative ... one that I certainly don't deserve.

Just to bring it all together, at present, Pilot Company:

- Operates 668 travel centers.
- Operates an additional 88 cardlocks, which are automated, unattended fueling sites designed for commercial fleet vehicles.
- Welcomes 1.3 million customers into our stores every day.
- Maintains 40 roadside assistance trucks; 1,107 company trucks; 5,294 showers; and 74,081 parking spots.
- Averages over $23 billion in annual revenue.

How did all this happen? First of all, a whole lot of luck came our way in the form of the eight breaks I just described. Secondly, it has been the result of the hard work of 28,000 Pilot team members.

Yes, these are the eight breaks that got us this far, but I know there are many more breaks to be had for the future of Pilot Company.

SECTION 2

REFLECTIONS

CHAPTER 7

WHAT REALLY MATTERS

Maximizing the Maxims

I SPENT THE FIRST PART OF THIS BOOK LAYING OUT THE BASIC TIME-line and narrative of my beginnings, as well as a brief history of Pilot. Throughout it all, I hope I have communicated more than just facts and details. After all, one's life cannot be separated from one's *philosophy* of life—the former will most definitely reflect the latter.

My point is that what we believe affects what we do, so we cannot just sum up our life stories with what we did or didn't do. What we do or don't do reflects what we consider to be important or unimportant in this life. To that end, though I referenced them in the first chapter, I would like to expound upon my own life maxims—the things I have come to believe and have found to be the most important.

As I said earlier, my son Bill asked me to compile these maxims years ago. It is my deepest desire that these maxims might someday serve to encourage and guide my family—and especially my grandchildren and great-grandchildren—for generations to come. I'm no philosopher or saint, but I am a man who knows he has been blessed beyond measure. So for a few pages, I would like to invite you into our family as I share what I believe matters most in this life.

Maxim I: Christian Belief

This is by far the most important of my life maxims. If an individual's whole life flows from his or her belief, then all the other maxims will follow. For me, *Christian belief* means believing in the Trinity, the Resurrection, and life everlasting. The Trinity is the Christian belief that God is expressed in three co-eternal persons: the Father, the Son, and the Holy Spirit.

Worshipping is so important as it is an outward and visible sign of your Christian belief. As an Episcopalian, we celebrate the Holy Communion at all our worship services. The breaking of bread and the drinking of wine symbolizes the sacrifice Christ made for us.

Prayer also must be an important part of an individual's life. I try to have a few minutes each day of prayer and reflection, and we never eat a meal without thanking God for all His gifts. Prayer is also so essential in times such as sickness, death, and other adversities.

My goal is to do everything I do and treat everyone I encounter in a Christian manner—which means treating them just as Christ treats me. The way I have been loved and forgiven by Christ is the way He expects me to love and treat others. Of course, I am a work-in-progress here. It is a wonderful thing that the whole cycle does not begin with me or my efforts but with Him and His finished work of proving his love for all of us at the Cross.

Maxim 2: Optimism

My second truism involves optimism. Optimists get more things done for more people for a very simple reason: positive attitudes almost always win. I'll be honest, I don't think anybody can accomplish much in this life without being an optimist. In my experience, I don't know any pessimistic people who get much done. Furthermore, I don't know of many pessimistic people whose company I even enjoy.

Someone who always tries to find and point out what's wrong with everything will generally succeed in doing so. And generally, they will make things fairly miserable for the rest of us. I don't know how much of this is about the personality we're born with and how much of it is learned by our experiences in life, but I hope our team will always find me remaining positive as much as possible in every situation. I don't always succeed, but this is my goal.

In fact, Natalie has told me that, at times, I probably need to be less optimistic and more realistic. I'm sure she's right, as usual. No, you shouldn't have blind optimism, but to me, the glass is never half empty— it's *always* half full. Likewise, it is never partly cloudy; it is partly sunny. Both perceptions are accurate, but only one leads to a more positive outlook, which I believe also leads to more positive results in life. After all, positive people get more done because they *believe they can.*

You have seen how much of our story has hinged on sports, business, and, as you will soon discover, politics. Quite frankly, if you enter an athletic contest and don't think you're going to win, then ninety-nine times out of a hundred, you won't. Similarly, in business, you have to stay confident in the mission and the plan you are pursuing, otherwise you'll fold the first time you fail or when something unexpectedly goes awry. Finally, if a person is running for political office and thinks a win is possible, then there's always a chance it will happen. If they don't, it will be reflected in every speech they give, every interview they grant, and ultimately, in every leadership decision they make.

> Someone who always tries to find and point out what's wrong with everything will generally succeed in doing so.

Stay positive. It is one of the most important parts of setting yourself up to win at what matters most, even before the game, business, or election has begun.

Maxim 3: Humility and Kindness

The third maxim is to be humble and kind, always remembering the less fortunate. In my experience, anyone who has achieved a modicum of success in business and who claims that he or she hasn't been lucky is either extremely exceptional or is not telling the truth. I have found the latter to be the more common case.

T. Boone Pickens, the legendary energy executive and one of America's best-known entrepreneurs, died recently. I once heard him say that he'd rather be *lucky* than *good*. Obviously, T. Boone Pickens was really good at what he did, but this sort of perspective lends itself to humility. In other words, if and when success comes, you should maintain the right heart—one that remembers everything isn't up to you.

Sometimes, you get more than you deserve from what you did. Sometimes, you get less.

> I want to be successful, but, more than this, I want to be humble.

I want to be successful, but, more than this, I want to be humble. I never want to look at my life and truly believe that I personally caused all the good outcomes I see around me. That is a dangerous, error-filled way to live that positions a human at the center of the universe, occupying a space only God can fill. As much as the human heart longs to be at the center of things, actually *being* at the center is heavy, draining, and ultimately robs you of both the joy of your successes and the lessons from your failures. Humility is not only the right posture because it's based upon a bedrock truth that everything doesn't hinge upon you, but it is also the posture that makes life most enjoyable.

In my opinion, kindness goes hand in hand with humility. It is a natural progression. If people aren't humble, then they may tend to think that success is all about their abilities, achievements, and accolades. And if they aren't successful, they may chase these things to the detriment of the people around them. When you see the world like this, people can become steppingstones to your success. And when you're stepping on people, you are far from being kind.

A humble attitude enables you to see other people's value and enjoy interacting with them toward a common goal. Instead of stepping *on* people, you will want to keep in step *with* them. You will want to see them succeed and prosper as much as you do. This is the essence of kindness: treating people the way you want to be treated. This is not a new concept. Start with humility and treat people with kindness...this is a recipe for success in the things that really matter most. It is so easy to be kind.

One more thought on this: I think it is important to be kind to everyone, not just to your closest friends or family. Kindness is not something you should pick and choose based upon the situation in which you find yourself. When we are kind only in certain situations, it's not *real* kindness because it flows from a place of self-preservation and personal gain rather than a principled attitude. If we are only kind when it benefits us to be so, our kindness will only be skin-deep.

Maxim 4: Family First

The fourth maxim is dear to me because it is about the *people* who are most dear to me: my family. I try to live by the adage that family must always come first. Everything else pales in comparison.

This is one of those expressions that most everyone touts, but not everyone lives. You would be hard-pressed to find a successful person in business (or in life) who would intentionally state that his or her family *doesn't* come first—and he or she would probably truly believe it. However, the key would be to find out what his or her family says about the matter.

It is easy to think you are putting your family first because of the time you spend working to provide for their needs and their future security. But in doing so, it is also easy to neglect what they *really* need: your time and attention. This damages your relationship with them in the future—the very future you *think* you are working so hard to create. There is no doubt that this is a balancing act, but it is one worth your constant energy because professional success alone cannot give you a completely fulfilled life. We *think* we know this, but the pace of our lives often reveals otherwise.

Sometimes, a frenetic pace may be necessary. But what *is never* necessary is neglecting your family along the way. We must endeavor to communicate to them—through our words, letters, texts, and time— *exactly* how much they mean to us. Don't leave it to chance, and don't assume they will fully grasp how valuable they are to you *today* simply because you told them *yesterday*. Just as each workday requires your full attention and effort, so does each day God has granted you the treasures of your marriage and family.

A few years ago, I had a friend in his sixties whose daughter passed away suddenly. Some time after she had passed, he said something to me that I have never forgotten. He said, "Every time you finish a conversation with your children, be sure to tell them that you love them. You never know how many more chances you will have to do so."

This is not just about death; it's about the real fullness of life. After all, what's the sense in accumulating money, winning a political race, or winning a ballgame if, after all the confetti falls and cheering subsides, you are left standing there with a broken family who never knew they mattered more than all of those other things?

Maxim 5: Politics

The fifth maxim is to get involved in the political process. Run for office. Or if you can't or don't feel that is right for you, seek out candidates you can support, raise money for, and work hard to get elected.

These days, politics is often something we complain about while watching from a distance. But I believe the right to vote brings with it a civic mandate to *exercise* that right. Alongside many other incredible men and women, I have served overseas in areas where freedom and democracy were (and often still are) in question. I think it is a dangerous thing for those of us who had these privileges for several generations to neglect them.

Yes, the system sometimes seems broken, which is why we need everyone to become involved in putting the right kind of people into office and holding the process accountable. This is our constitutional right and privilege, so it shouldn't be left to others to uphold. We each have a part to play.

I will share more stories from my experience in the political arena in greater detail in the chapters to come. For now, I would simply encourage everyone—including you—either to run for some kind of office or support a candidate in his or her campaign. It doesn't have to be a high office, either. The person who serves on the local school board is just as important as the one who represents us in the United States Senate. Each level of government plays a critical role in the cohesion of a free and democratic society.

> Yes, the system sometimes seems broken, which is why we need everyone to become involved in putting the right kind of people into office and holding the process accountable.

It's easy to be a critic, but good people can help fix broken systems; they just have to get involved and do so from the inside. Throwing rocks from the outside or turning a blind eye is not going to help.

Maxim 6: Set the Example (and Change Is a Must)

The sixth maxim calls us to always strive to set a good example. It may sound like a cliché, but it never will stop being true. People may be independent beings, but rarely do we independently make decisions, accomplish tasks, or engage in important activities. We do so in groups. In some ways, we are like pack animals, leaning into and finding purpose in community. For better or worse, we will follow the example of those ahead of us. And in return, someone behind us will follow our example.

I was privileged to have people like General Neyland set the example for me. By now, you have seen how much his influence has affected not only my decisions *in* life, but also my outlook *on* life. They say integrity is what you do when no one is watching; this is true, but remember that just because you can't see them doesn't mean someone isn't watching. Someone is *always* watching, so do what's right not just because it's right, but also because you want to set the right example.

Imagine I, as the leader, tell my team members to come to work at 8:00 a.m., and yet I consistently show up at 8:30. No matter what I am *telling them*, I am *showing them* what is really important to me. Generally, things don't simply *happen to us* randomly, but we often act as if they do. If your organization consistently receives negative feedback from customers, constant turnover from disgruntled employees, and a perpetual failure to meet financial goals, then it is doubtful these results are completely random. Yes, there are seasons when bad things just happen to businesses and families. But if the trends are constant over years and years, it is probably not *just happening*; the leaders are more likely doing something that is *contributing*, if not directly *causing*, the negativity. You are already leading by example whether you know it or not and whether that example is a good one or not. Make sure it's a good one.

Along these lines, a leader must understand that he or she will most often set an example through some sort of change. People often fear change, striving to keep the status quo so as not to rock the boat. But a good leader will be an agent of change because he or she realizes change is a must. Change is coming whether you embrace it or not. You cannot stop change from happening, but you will be remiss if you don't embrace it with wisdom, excellence, and foresight to maximize it for the good of the company and your team. It is better to make a salad out of your laurels than to rest on them.

Here at Pilot, change is our friend, not our enemy. If we had not been willing to change throughout the course of our many decades in this industry, we would still be trying to sell only gas and cigarettes. Consequently, we'd be out of business. We eventually had to change so we could get into the convenience store business, but this wasn't where we needed to stay forever. We wouldn't be half the company we are today if we hadn't gotten in the travel center business. In other words, we can't just change once; change must be a living part of our culture.

Who knows what changes are to come for Pilot Company? A culture that is open to change is necessary for leaders to set the right example for their companies—and for their families. If you don't fear change and stop running from it, change will be your friend. Otherwise, it will be your worst enemy.

Maxim 7: Integrity

The seventh maxim is to always do the right thing, being faithful and accountable in every way. I have already said that integrity means doing the right thing when no one is around to see it or praise you for it. In today's world, we seem to spend quite a bit of time debating what is right and wrong, but I think in most situations, the difference is pretty easy to distinguish.

Here are some telltale signs that something is the right thing to do: it will usually be the hardest of the choices at hand. It will probably require you to work more diligently and to communicate more fully and openly with those working alongside you. Also, it might not always lead to the highest gain on the bottom line.

Don't cut corners to maximize profits. Those corners maintain the integrity of the shape of your business, so honor them. Money will take care of itself if you take care of doing business in the right way, treating people well, and honoring the principles that reflect your core beliefs. Stay accountable to all these things and, when you make a mistake (which you will), admit it and try to correct it. If that's what we'd like others to do, we must be ready to do it ourselves.

Maxim 8: Keep It Simple

The eighth maxim is to keep it simple. Good leaders always seek to simplify things rather than complicate them. This is not to say the situations we face in life and business are not sometimes extremely complicated. Of course, they are. This is more about *disposition* than *execution*; that is, a leader should always keep the main thing the main thing, which will, in turn, create a sense of clarity and confidence in the decision-making process. Sometimes there are dozens of good solutions that can be picked. A simple understanding of what matters most to an individual or company will help narrow down options to keep everyone and everything pointed in the same direction.

I love technology, but it can be complicated. My smartwatch can tell me my heart rate, as well as whether I am in atrial fibrillation. With nothing but an oral command, it can show me a picture of my wife or tell me the weather forecast for China. It can track my whereabouts from a satellite in space, order food for me from a local restaurant, and, yes, it can even tell me the time.

My watch is complicated, and complicated technology or processes have their place in *some areas* of life. But what we do in life and business should be pretty simple. Keeping your personal and organizational goals and values in mind and constantly reinforced to those you lead can help declutter the process when things get murky and overly complex.

Maxim 9: Health, Exercise, Alcohol, and Drugs

The ninth maxim is very practical, but also very important to the process of living healthily in all aspects of life. It begins with being faithful to keep up your physical fitness. If you don't keep yourself *in shape*, many other things in your life will tend to get bent *out of shape*. It is important to work out consistently in some manner. Run, walk, ride a bicycle (inside or outside), or do whatever personally appeals to you. Whatever you do, make sure it contributes to a good cardio program to keep your heart healthy.

The scale only shows you one metric of your health, and people can become obsessed with the seesaw of watching ounces and pounds rise and fall. This is a trap. Don't become obsessed with the number on the scale, but don't become lackadaisical about it, either. I monitor my weight as a part of my total health. If it gets out of hand, I don't panic and jump into yo-yo dieting; rather, I simply try to make sensible choices for the long haul. In this way, good health becomes and remains a lifestyle, not an occasional novelty.

I also cannot overemphasize the importance of getting plenty of sleep. Sleep is one of the most measurable factors that contribute to longevity in life. People who sleep well live longer; it's that simple. So work hard to rest well.

When it comes to alcohol, I should mention that I have never had a single drink in all my eighty-nine years. I'm not saying you *must* abstain as I have chosen to do, but I do recommend moderation at the very least. I have seen too many lives, marriages, and businesses ruined by alcohol abuse. One reason I have never had a drink is that I have personally always wanted to be in control of my actions and intellect during whatever situation that might come up. For example, imagine you were drinking, and something bad happened to one of your children or a friend. They might need your immediate help. How would you feel if you weren't able to respond appropriately due to a clouded mind? You might think I'm being a bit dramatic here, but this state of readiness has never done me wrong. Needless to say, there are some real advantages to avoiding alcohol.

While moderation may be acceptable for alcohol, illegal/recreational drugs and tobacco should *never* be used. Drugs are a one-way street to disaster. And though it is legal, it would be best for your health to completely abstain from tobacco. I have never used any of these in almost ninety years, which, by God's grace, has probably helped me be able to see almost ninety years of life.

Maxim 10: Work Hard and Have a Purpose to Your Life

There is no substitute for hard work. And if you're going to be working hard, it is important to do so toward a purpose that matters.

I have many fond memories of the late, great Lady Vols basketball coach, Pat Summit. Of the many incredible things she said and did, I will never forget her saying, "Don't ever let anyone outwork you." It is such a simple takeaway, but if each of us were to do it, we'd all stay busy for the rest of our lives.

As I have told you, I know I'm not the smartest or most capable person in the world. I fully expect that someone out there will outsmart me or do something better than I can. But let it never be said that someone has outworked me. We can't control how talented, intelligent, or intuitive we are, but we *can* control how hard we work. Think about that: hard work is one of the only things in this life that you can actually control and affect. Even if it doesn't make you monetarily rich, being a hard worker is a rich way to live your life, so never let yourself be outworked.

> Even if it doesn't make you monetarily rich, being a hard worker is a rich way to live your life, so never let yourself be outworked.

This doesn't necessarily mean that work is what you have to do all the time. After all, time is your most important asset, so working smart is just as important as working hard. Or, better said, *working smart is the best way to work hard.* If you physically work hard but do not also have intentional strategies that keep addressing your overall culture and objectives, then working hard may not be enough. You can work hard by hacking at a tree with a dull hatchet for an hour, or you can work smart by spending your first twenty minutes sharpening the hatchet.

The other key here is to own and embrace a purpose in life. Work, in and of itself, is not a sustainable purpose, even though it can be all-consuming. You don't want to be completely consumed by something that cannot completely fulfill your life. That is not a good trade. Without a true purpose, you can just rock along, work hard, and enjoy yourself. People do it all the time; never has it been easier to do so as it is these days when life is lived at such a breakneck pace. It is all too easy to put your head down and stay busy doing things that don't make a difference for you or anyone else beyond the paycheck you receive for doing them.

As you work, you must always return to the question of purpose. This is not to say that life won't require a lot of tedious, mundane effort. It will. But the time will come when purpose will be a necessity, when you need a better reason for going to work than simply earning an income. That's when you'll start asking yourself what you're going to do to help other people and how you'll make this a better world. These are key questions—questions you shouldn't wait to answer. Jobs and tasks will always be changing, so let purpose be your constant.

Maxim II: Passion

The penultimate maxim, passion, flows out of purpose. Be passionate in what you are doing, whether it's your job, working in the community, or your play. You can do anything, but I don't believe you can do anything *well* without passion.

We always tell our team members that, if they don't like working here, they ought to go work someplace else. This is not meant to sound mean or dismissive; quite the contrary. We genuinely don't want people to work at anything—including the work our team does here at Pilot— that they can't stand doing. Yes, as leaders, we could still extract hours and tasks out of them to make this company grow, but at what cost? If we don't care about the people who work for us and their passions in life, then we run the risk of throwing out one of our important purposes, which is to serve our team members well.

It is often said that life is too short to be doing something you don't enjoy. While I agree with this, I think life will often require you to do things you don't enjoy; we all know this to be true. So how do you balance the *pursuit* of passion and the reality that some things will try to *steal* that passion? I have found that attitude can affect one's enjoyment of the task more than the task itself. A man with a positive attitude can enjoy something as laborious and simple as digging a ditch, especially if he remembers his higher purposes as he digs it.

That said, I believe we are each made differently and should do our best to put people into positions that fit well with their personalities and abilities. Consequently, people are more likely to enjoy themselves when they are aligned with what they are passionate about doing. You would never want the person who hates math to be in charge of accounting or the person who hates having dirty hands servicing the trucks. It is not only doubtful that they would do well in positions that are misaligned to their proclivities, it is also doubtful they will enjoy them at all. It's a lose-lose.

Here is a fresh take on the matter: life is too short to be constantly working at things you *can't* enjoy. Again, you may learn to enjoy doing things you originally hated, but otherwise, don't spend you whole life doing something that drains the life from you. If you have to work in an area that you don't enjoy, then try to find other things outside of work that you *do* enjoy.

Maybe you have a passion to serve. If so, find opportunities to work or volunteer in the community or in nonprofit agencies. Perhaps your passion will be reflected in delivering mobile meals or feeding the homeless. I've found that nothing magnifies my passion more than seeing how others can benefit from it.

And do not neglect your passions outside of work, family, and service. Your passion can *and should* lead to plenty of play, as well. It is important to have things in life that you enjoy *just for the sake of doing them*. Play golf. Play tennis. Go skiing. Add to life those things that interest you because—and the saying is accurate—life is short.

Maxim 12: Give Back

The final maxim puts feet to the beliefs, philosophies, and insights of the others: we must give back.

This list of maxims began with *Christian Belief*, which is the only maxim more important to me than this last one. To that end, a Scripture that truly affects the outlook of my life is Luke 12:48. This is one of those verses that people tend to use, but often inadvertently misquote— and doing so is *big* miss. People quote the verse as, "To whom much is given, much is *expected*." This sounds right and even noble, but if you really crack open the Good Book, you'll see this is not what this passage actually says. Rather, it reads, "Everyone to whom much was given, of him much will be *required*" (Luke 12:48 ESV, emphasis mine).

There is a big difference between something that is *expected* and something that is *required*. I know that we have been given much, and I believe God has given it to us for reasons only known to Him. I *don't know* why He has blessed our family and business in this way. I *do know* that He requires us to use these resources for His higher purposes. It may sound restricting to some people, but giving because you know it is required is actually quite liberating. It removes the question from the equation, freeing you to just do it.

Though it may sound counterintuitive, the happiest people I know are not those who *receive* the most, but rather those who *give* the most. In terms of money, you get to decide how much and to whom you will give. The biblical tithe is ten percent of your income; I believe that should be a *minimum*. I think you should most certainly give to your church, but it doesn't have to stop there. Give to social causes, education, or the arts— there are so many worthy causes that will bring you enjoyment when you let go of something in your hands and put it into someone else's.

A good friend of ours, Dan Matthews, the longtime Rector of our church, St. John's in Knoxville, used to tell the story about listening to a psychologist speak at a clergy conference. After his presentation, he asked the audience for questions. One lady raised her hand and said, "One of my best friends is about to have a nervous breakdown. What can I do for her?"

The doctor said, "Nothing." There was complete silence. Then he said, "Get her to do something for somebody else." There are definitely extenuating circumstances and situations that will require varied approaches, but, in general, I think he was right. Doing for others does something for you. In my experience, the people who do things for other people are the healthiest and the happiest people among us.

I want to be one of them.

No list of maxims is complete and each person will express what is important in life in different ways. However, I truly believe that these twelve concepts cover most of the critical areas of life as they relate to one's attitude and actions. For what it's worth, attitudes always lead to actions, so it is important that each of us focus on what we truly believe to be important so that our life's pursuits will reflect something intentional and substantial. I hope that a few of my thoughts might encourage you as you pursue the unique opportunities in your own life.

CHAPTER 8

POLITICS

Engagement Matters

As you know, I believe it is essential that we each engage in the political process in some form or fashion. This is the privilege—and thus, in my opinion, the duty—of every citizen of a free nation. We will not all run for office or occupy extremely influential positions, but we can all be influential in one way or another, and it can start by getting involved in local politics in our hometowns.

My views on political engagement are not just theoretical; they come from a lifetime of experiences in the political arena. Over the years, I have had the honor of being directly in the fray with some incredible individuals who not only shaped policy and life for local, state, or federal government, but also for me personally.

I'd like to share a few memories and insights about several of them.

Howard Baker

My journey through politics began with Howard Baker. Back in 1963, the Pilot offices were in downtown Knoxville in the Greater Tennessee Building. Right across the hall were the law offices of Morton and Lewis. George Morton, one of the principal partners, caught me in the hallway as I was coming back from lunch one day and said, "Howard Baker's coming by here. He's thinking about running for the Senate."

I had met Howard several times, but I did not really know him that well. Even so, the whole idea of him running for the State Senate intrigued me, so I went across the hall to speak with him on the matter. I knew he would have to be running against the State Senator, Fred Berry, from south Knoxville. Fred owned a funeral home and was a colorful politician, often considered controversial. I asked Howard what his thoughts were about running against Fred Berry.

"Fred Berry?" he replied. "Jim, I'm thinking about running for the *United States* Senate."

I remember this moment so very distinctly. It was inconceivable to me that somebody I knew could possibly be a member of the U.S. Senate. It was one of those moments when my little world got a little bit bigger. This is what the political process does for us: it broadens our horizons as we help broaden the horizons of others who are served and whose lives are improved through the democratic process.

> It was inconceivable to me that somebody I knew could possibly be a member of the U.S. Senate.

Sure enough, Howard ran for the Senate for the first time in 1964, which was the year Senator Barry Goldwater lost by a landslide to the incumbent President Lyndon Johnson. Howard was running to fill the unexpired term of Senator Estes Kefauver, a Democrat who died in office earlier in 1963. Howard's opponent was Congressman Ross Bass.

Howard was narrowly defeated. Though he lost, the fact that it was by a narrow margin was noteworthy because, in those days in the South, it was nearly impossible for any Republican to win any sort of popular election. This region of the country tended to vote strictly blue. Baker lost to Bass by a mere 4.7 percentage points, which was the closest any Republican had come to being popularly elected to the Senate from the state of Tennessee.

Two years later, Howard would have the chance to try again.

In 1966, Howard Baker ran for the same Senate seat again, but this time, his opponent was the sitting Governor of Tennessee, Frank Clement. Clement beat out Bass in the Democratic primary to lock up his party's nomination, which, in general, meant a lock on the general election.

But Howard proved to be a more formidable opponent than anyone expected. He campaigned hard while Clement failed to mobilize his own base. When the dust settled and the votes were tallied, Howard Baker was elected as the first Republican Senator from Tennessee since Reconstruction, as well as the first Republican in Tennessee to be popularly elected to the Senate.

He would go on to win again in 1972 and 1978, becoming a mainstay in the Senate and earning a reputation in Washington as "The Great Conciliator." He was known for sticking to his promises—promises he made because of his personal values and the integrity he sought to foster and promote throughout the nation. When Howard Baker really believed in something and considered it to be the right thing to do, he was known to reach across the aisle to broker compromises, regardless of the political consequences.

Such integrity would play into his story later—and also greatly affect the way I see politics.

Howard's Press Secretary was Ron McMahan so they obviously traveled together often. Ron started off as a reporter for the old *Knoxville Journal*. After the election, he moved to Washington to work for Senator Baker but eventually came back to become the owner and Editor-in-Chief of the *Knoxville Journal*, which was eventually sold to Gannett.

Ron and I spent a lot of time together working on Senator Baker's various campaigns, so I had a front-row seat to his fun character. During Howard's run for reelection in 1972, I met Howard and Ron at the Tri-Cities airport near the eastern border of Tennessee so we could ride together to a fundraiser in the little town of Elizabethton. We were trying to make it there in plenty of time; however, the road was narrow and crowded, which meant we needed to make up for lost time.

Ron was driving, Howard was sitting in the front seat, and I was sitting in the back. All of a sudden, blue lights and a siren begin flashing and blaring behind us as a state trooper pulled us over. This was not ideal for sure, but I had no idea just how ready Ron really was for such a situation.

After he pulled the car to the shoulder, Ron jumped out and began yelling at the state trooper, "Are you Senator Baker's escort? Where have you been?"

Looking very flustered, the poor officer replied in a panic, "No, sir, but I will be!" Just as quickly as Ron had exited the car, both he and the trooper got back inside their respective cars and we received a police escort to our event that night.

There were many funny stories like this on the campaign trail with Howard, but the story that still affects me the most to this day isn't really funny; rather, it exemplifies what kind of person Howard really was. In 1978, he was running for the Senate for the last time and I was his Finance Chairman. At the time, he was the Minority Leader of the Senate. He would go on become the Majority Leader after the Republicans took control in the 1980 elections.

Needless to say, by this point Howard was a popular figure in politics, which meant my job was fairly simple. It was easy to raise money for a guy with his name recognition and good reputation. The fundraising campaign was bringing in donations from all over the country and everybody was patting me on the back for my efforts. The truth was that it didn't take much effort.

But then everything changed—and I also discovered what kind of man Howard Baker really was. President Jimmy Carter was pushing to sign a treaty to eventually sell the Panama Canal back to the Panamanians and then lease its use from them. It was a hotbed issue that divided the political landscape and, for the most part, the Republicans on the far right very much opposed the treaty.

Imagine their shock and horror, then, when the Republican minority leader of the Senate came out in favor of the treaty. It sent shockwaves throughout the party and suddenly, the money that had been flowing like milk and honey dried up.

As his Finance Chairman, I was obviously alarmed. I called Ron and requested a meeting with the Senator. It turned out that Howard was coming to Huntsville, Tennessee that weekend, so Ron invited me down to have lunch with him on the upcoming Saturday.

I got there about 11:30 a.m., just as Howard was finishing up a game of tennis with three of his old buddies—banker Bill Swain and lawyers Don Stansberry and Bob Worthington. After his friends walked away, Howard and I stood alone. Mind you, I have since shrunk a bit in these recent years, but they used to call me "Big Jim," mainly because I was six feet, four inches tall. Howard, on other hand, stood only about five feet, seven inches.

> After he pulled the car to the shoulder, Ron jumped out and began yelling at the state trooper, "Are you Senator Baker's escort? Where have you been?"

I was worried about his support of the treaty and the subsequent drop in donations, and I planned to let Howard know about it in no uncertain terms. "Senator," I said, "we really need to talk about this Panama Canal thing because it's killing our fundraising."

He looked at me and said, "Jim, sit down." His tone was very blunt.

I sat down and he proceeded to educate me on the matter at hand. It soon became very clear that I was no longer the taller man in this conversation. I sat there looking up at him. "Jim, let me tell you about the Constitution. Our forefathers were some of the most intelligent people who ever lived, and their wisdom is still pervasive today. They intentionally created a Congress in which members of the House of Representatives would be elected only for two years, while senators would have six years. Do you know why they did that, Jim?"

I could have answered the question, but I didn't dare…and he didn't wait for me to try.

"I'll tell you why, Jim. They wanted Senators to have the security of six years during which they were free of the politics of seeking reelection. This allowed the House to be able to look at more current matters and the Senate to be free to make decisions that really affect the long-term welfare of the nation."

I didn't come for a lesson in civics, but his passion could not be denied. Besides, I knew I was receiving infinite wisdom—just as if one of the Founding Fathers himself were offering it.

> **I had been looking up at him the entire time, but never before had I looked up to him quite so much.**

He continued, "They gave the Senate the power to approve treaties just like this one. It is my job to take a step back and really look at how this affects people for the long haul—and that's just what I've been doing. I have consulted every former President, every former Secretary of State, and everyone else I can find who has dedicated time and research to this matter—and they *all* say this is the right thing to do. So I'm going to vote for it."

He took a breath, then concluded, "Now, if all of this is okay with you, Jim, and you want to keep on raising money for us, then let's go have lunch. But if you want to stop because of my decision, that's fine too. We're still friends either way."

I had been looking up *at him* the entire time, but never before had I looked up *to him* quite so much.

"Let's go have lunch," I said.

Howard suffered dire political consequences in the aftermath of his decision to go against the wishes of his own party. In the 1980 election, he ran against Ronald Reagan and George H. W. Bush for the Republican presidential nomination, but he never had a fighting chance. Howard Baker's chief political aspiration had always been becoming

President, but still, he never regretted his decision to perform his duty and, more importantly, do what he believed to be the right thing for the country, regardless of the fallout.

Howard went on to become the Chief of Staff for Ronald Reagan, and eventually, the U.S. Ambassador to Japan. I will never forget the time Bill Sansom and I flew to Washington to see him about a Knoxville Chamber of Commerce matter. We went into the White House to meet with Howard and, after a few minutes of catching up together in his office, he unexpectedly blurted out, "Well, let's go see the President."

The next thing I knew, we were standing in the Oval Office posing for a picture with President Ronald Reagan. Once again, the question must be asked: *how did this happen?* In this case, it happened because of the right kind of friend. This experience epitomized exactly what it was like to be a friend of Howard Baker: he always exceeded expectations in serving those around him. He greatly affected my viewpoint of politics but also my view of life itself. He taught me the importance of doing the right thing in everything I do.

Lamar Alexander

Howard enriched my life not just through all I learned from him but also through many of the people I met because of my friendship with him. One such person was Lamar Alexander.

Lamar had been a legislative assistant to Howard when he was in the Senate, and we met through this mutual connection. The first time I ever talked to Lamar, he asked me to raise money for him—he was that confident about what he wanted to do to serve and why he wanted to do it. Of course, I said yes.

I began helping raise support for Lamar when he ran for Governor of Tennessee in 1974. He lost that election, but he wouldn't be deterred by the setback. He ran again in 1978 and won, defeating Democratic candidate and Knoxville banker Jake Butcher.

Lamar served as the Governor of Tennessee for two terms. He taught me something interesting about the differences in running for an executive political office versus a legislative office. He pointed out that once you are elected to the House or the Senate, the people who supported you—that is, influencers who worked hard and raised money to help you get elected—tend to want you to pass legislation related to what they care about the most. This is common in the democratic process: people support those who will make decisions that reflect their own values and interests.

But when you run for an executive position like Mayor, Governor, or President, things are a bit different. Because of the sheer breadth of such an office and its responsibilities, the people who helped you get there will be people you will have to call upon to serve in your cabinet or administration. If you want to succeed, you will not just let them sit back and expect you to work for their interests; you will bring them to work alongside you for the interests of everyone under your collective charge.

When you invest money in the right kind of people and help get them elected to office, the invaluable return on that investment is good government.

This changes the way you look at the people you ask to fundraise and campaign for you. You are not just raising money; you are also raising up future leaders and, as we have learned, the head leader rises or falls on his or her ability to put the right leaders in the right places. Politics, just like business and football, is a team sport—if, that is, you actually want to win. And by *win*, I mean do something for the greater good, not just win an election.

Lamar also taught me a lot about giving and philanthropy. I will discuss my thoughts on these topics in an upcoming chapter, but many of my philosophies came from Lamar's influence. He helped me see that all giving is not the same. People tend to think of generosity only in the realm of charity, nonprofits, or worthy philanthropic causes—and I am certainly in favor of giving generously to each of these. I believe in giving to your church, the United Way, and a host of other organizations and endeavors because it is the right thing to do.

But there is another way that giving one's dollars can greatly affect the common good. When you invest money in the right kind of people and help get them elected to office, the invaluable return on that investment is good government. Since it is sometimes eclipsed by the negativity that surrounds so much of our political process these days, we can all too easily forget that our Founding Fathers established this government not as a way to rule over or dominate people, but rather as a protection and an accurate expression *of the people*. This includes benefits, of course, that trickle down *for the people* and are administered *by the people*.

I believe not just in voting for my favorite candidate, but also in being invested in the process of helping him or her get elected—not for the sake of what they can do for me or people like me but because I believe our Founding Fathers were right: good government is good for all the people under its service.

Lamar's time as Governor opened the door for one of the highest honors of my life in the realm of service: I was appointed to the University of Tennessee Board of Trustees. This gave me the opportunity to directly serve, protect, and enrich the university that has meant so much to me for so much of my life.

Lamar's second term as Governor expired at the end of 1987, after which he became the President of the University of Tennessee in 1988. He served in this position for only three years. President George H. W. Bush soon called upon him to serve in another important role: Secretary of Education. After his time in Bush's cabinet, he toyed with the idea of running for president, but it never panned out. Instead, Lamar eventually ran for the Senate seat vacated by retiring Senator Fred Thompson. Lamar won the seat and then won two subsequent reelections.

As his final reelection bid drew to a close in 2014, the campaign was in need of extra funding. He hired a professional fundraiser whose plan was to put Lamar and me on calls together to prospective donors. We went to our house at Blackberry Farm on a Friday afternoon and placed about ten or fifteen calls. Lamar started the calls and gave "the talk," and then I made the pitch for donations. When it was all said and done, Lamar said we raised about half a million dollars in thirty minutes, which was by far the greatest, most efficient fundraising story of my life. The best part was that I experienced it, along with many other adventures, alongside a dear friend in Lamar Alexander.

Lamar served in the U.S. Senate for eighteen years before finally retiring from the Senate in 2020, and I was honored to work with him during that entire time.

Presidential Experiences

Running in these political circles with Lamar and Howard caused me and my family to segue into raising money for other politicians, including President Reagan, President George H. W. Bush (41), and President George W. Bush (43). This is generally how fundraising and political campaigns work: party members help one another campaigning and fundraising toward the common goal of getting as many party candidates elected as possible, which increases their chances of being more effective when they take office.

We became more involved with the Reagans and the Bushes because we saw the kind of people they were. It was very evident that they cared deeply about the country—and again, we were able to positively affect the lives of our fellow citizens by getting behind the candidates we believed would serve people well.

When Howard was Chief of Staff for President Reagan, Natalie and I were invited to a state dinner being held for the Chancellor of Austria. There were a number of famous people there, including Maria von Trapp, about whom *The Sound of Music* was written. Also in attendance was the coach of the Superbowl Champion Washington Redskins, Joe Gibbs.

The entrance into the event was extremely formal. All of the guests waited in a holding room off to the side until our names were called. The press would then take photographs of the person of importance who was being announced and was entering the White House ballroom with pomp. It was very prestigious.

"Mr. and Mrs. Joe Gibbs of Washington," announced the attendant. Cameras began flashing left and right as Coach Gibbs and his wife made their appearance before the media. We were next. This was going to be fun! We stepped up to the threshold and prepared for our lofty intro-duction to the world.

"Mr. and Mrs. James Haslam of Knoxville." We glided into the room, but I am not joking when I tell you that not a single flash of a single camera went off. There wasn't even a *courtesy flash*! We laugh about it to this day.

> We glided into the room, but I am not joking when I tell you that not a single flash of a single camera went off. There wasn't even a courtesy flash!

Another time, we were attending a White House dinner during the George W. Bush administration. By that point, they didn't really do the whole picture/introduction thing as much anymore, for which we were grateful. Instead, we attended a cocktail hour in the West Wing. There were about sixty of us there at the time, and we were supposed to mingle until they called us into the dining room.

Natalie and I wanted to be friendly, so we made our way over to talk to one couple who was standing alone. We made first-name introduc-tions and were talking for a bit, Natalie to the lady and I to the gentleman. I found out that he was from Michigan but lived in Washington. I asked him how long he had lived there, and he said they had been in the city for about twenty years. He asked what I did for a living; it was very nice of him to ask. I told him and, to reciprocate his courtesy, I asked what he did.

"Well, I'm a Supreme Court Justice."

"Oh."

As it turned out, we had been chatting with Associate Justice John Paul Stevens, who served on the nation's highest court from 1975 until 2010. It just goes to show you that you never know who you're talking to, especially when you're in Washington.

Justice Stevens might have thought it odd that we didn't know who *he* was, but we've always been perfectly content for people to not know who *we* are. Washington is the kind of town wherein standing out is often *not* a good thing. Natalie learned this lesson the hard way at another state dinner. The master of ceremonies kept offering toasts for various officials and dignitaries in the room, which meant we had to keep standing up each time to join in the applause. The thing was that every time she stood up, she knocked over her tiny chair. Natalie has a quiet, gentle demeanor, so she never wants to make any kind of a scene or fuss, which means we get an especially good laugh out of this memory.

Without missing a beat, he laughed and said, "Well, I'm just glad you didn't wear the same underwear!"

Who knew that Natalie Haslam would be the type to repeatedly throw chairs in the White House?

Finally, one of our favorite presidential memories comes from one of the most famous elections in American history in the year 2000. When the voting results originally came in, the election was called for Senator Al Gore of Tennessee. However, a dispute arose regarding Florida, and the election was then called for Bush instead.

The bottom line was that there was a razor-thin margin between the two candidates, which meant a recount had to be held in Florida. This was when phrases like "hanging chads" and "pregnant chads" entered into the American lexicon, referring to paper ballots and their indentations from the voting machines that had failed to definitively punch all the way through, leaving their official results in dispute.

The citizens of the nation waited on the edge of their seats for several weeks as the election results hung in the balance. I had worn a particular tie on the night of the election, and I wasn't about to *stop* wearing it until we found out whether or not the candidate we had worked so hard to help get into office had officially won. As you probably know, it finally came down to a vote of the House of Representatives and, sure enough, George W. Bush became the forty-third President of the United States. A few months into his administration, we visited him in the White House, and I told him the story about wearing my tie every day until the results were official.

Without missing a beat, he laughed and said, "Well, I'm just glad you didn't wear the same underwear!"

Bill Haslam

I really can't talk about my experiences in politics without talking about my son Bill Haslam. I am a man who has been blessed beyond measure with children who engage in worthwhile endeavors, but who, more importantly, love and serve their families extremely well. It really never mattered to me that my children accomplish things that society will consider important or impressive; it only mattered that my children became people of faith, integrity, and hard work.

And they all have.

I could brag on all my children (and often do), but since this chapter is specifically about politics, I want to share some stories about Bill's political journey to date. Oddly enough, when they were young men, it was Jimmy, not Bill, who was always involved in politics. Jimmy's college roommate was a young man named Bob Corker. Bob became and has remained a close, personal friend to our family for many years. He became the Mayor of Chattanooga and eventually a U.S. Senator.

Believe it or not, it was Bob, Jimmy's roommate, who first planted the seeds of politics in Bill's life.

Bill and his wife, Crissy, were vacationing in Destin, Florida, when they randomly bumped into Bob at dinner. Bob is an avid runner and cyclist, so he invited Bill to join him for a bike ride the next morning. Bill accepted and, while they were together, Bob told Bill that he should run for Mayor of Knoxville because the current Mayor, Victor Ashe, was term-limited and would soon be leaving office. At first, the idea was completely foreign to Bill. "Why would I ever want to do that?" he asked.

Bob told him all about his own prior experiences in business and how being Mayor opened up so many bigger opportunities to do good and help people on a grander scale. Bill is a quiet man, and it appeared that he wasn't interested, but the idea just wouldn't stop rolling around in his head.

When he returned to Knoxville, we sat down and talked about it. I was shocked he was even considering it. Again, I always thought that if any of my children were to run for office, it would be Jimmy. Even so, I encouraged him that if he really wanted to try it, he should go for it. He had my full support.

Bill entered the mayoral race and took the plunge into politics, not knowing all the places it would lead him. I had been involved in many political races over the years, but mainly only in fundraising endeavors. I consider this to be the *wholesale* side of politics. But when someone in our immediate family actually ran for office, we entered the *retail* side of politics.

The differences between the two were many, but, above all, retail politics require you to get out into the field to shake hands and actually interact with people. It is about sincerely listening and understanding what is going on in people's lives and in their communities. Being extremely intelligent and thoughtful, Bill acclimated to these kinds of tasks quite well.

One night, our team was engaged in a kind of "boiler room" operation. We had a list of people who had voted in previous elections, and we were cold-calling them to talk about their opportunity to elect Bill Haslam as Mayor. Along with Bill, there were about fifteen of us present. Our strategy involved making the standard pitch, but if someone had a question, we would call Bill over to let him speak directly to the voter on the call. It was a lot of work, but it was good work because it meant actually talking to—and listening to—real people.

On one call in particular, someone asked about some kind of skateboarding park in North Knoxville. We didn't have a clue about it, but when Bill caught wind of the conversation, he insisted on taking the call. To our surprise, he began talking all about the prospective plans and locations for the project. When he hung up, I asked, "Bill, how did you know about that?"

"Well," he replied, "when you go out and knock on so many doors, you hear about things. I was in a neighborhood just the other day, and they were talking all about this skateboard park." I was proud that my son had taught me such a valuable lesson: if you're running for political office, you must get out and *engage* the people and not just to *secure their votes*. You have to actually listen to them, regardless of whether or not they give you their support.

During Bill's mayoral campaign, meeting people in the community became a family affair. We all chipped in to get out and canvas every neighborhood in Knoxville. It was hard work, but we made memories I wouldn't trade for anything.

While Bill is fairly mild-mannered, his brother, Jimmy, lacks anything resembling a delicate approach—even in campaigning. We were knocking on doors in West Knoxville when Jimmy began speaking with a family he had known for quite some time. He was asking how their elderly father was doing when their father himself slowly began walking down the hallway to join in the conversation. When Jimmy noticed he was older than he remembered, he asked, "How old are you now, sir?"

"Eighty-two," the man replied.

"Well, early voting starts Monday!" Jimmy replied.

Despite funny interactions like this, Bill still won that election and served two terms as the Mayor of Knoxville. He never lost his desire to listen and serve the people's interest above his own. Politics can be a difficult business because everyone feels their own interests are most important. It is a leader's job to somehow balance all the competing interests and complaints in order to find a common ground that will best serve the good of the whole. As you can imagine, there is no way to please everyone all the time. That's the reality for any leader.

Serving in any position of leadership—and especially a political position—exposes you to more people, which in turn opens you up to more criticism. During and after Bill's mayoral campaigns, I became aware that some people had negative things to say about our family. They acted as if the fact that Bill was Mayor would somehow mean everything I wanted to do in the community would suddenly come to pass. It has always been an easy indictment, though some do more than just imply it. Many people will say it to your face. I understand that deep involvement in the community and in politics brings along with it this kind of thing.

There are a few things that have always stuck out to me that seem to counter this sometimes less-than-subtle assumption about me and my family. We have attended St. John's Episcopal Cathedral in downtown Knoxville for many years. The main entrance we go in and out of is on the west side of the property next to a curb that lacks proper drainage. For years, every time it rains, water pools at this entrance and it is a real eyesore, as well as a headache to navigate.

There is also a stoplight just up the hill from Neyland Drive by the City-County Building that clogs up the flow of traffic on Sundays, even though there is very little traffic coming the other way. It is a nuisance that could easily be remedied by simply reprogramming the stoplight to flash red on Sundays so drivers don't have to wait so long.

When Bill took office, I actually mentioned these two things to our new Mayor, suggesting that he get the drainage issue taken care of and that he get someone to program the light to blink on Sundays. These things were not just good for me; they would help everyone who came to our church or drove down that particular road on Sundays.

I'm here to inform you that Bill was Mayor for nearly eight years and to this day, many years afterwards, that puddle is still there, and that light does not blink on Sundays. For all the conspiracy theories about nepotism, I couldn't even get my own son to fix a mud puddle on my behalf!

For all the conspiracy theories about nepotism, I couldn't even get my own son to fix a mud puddle on my behalf!

Bill Haslam was too busy actually serving the greater good of the city of Knoxville, as he should have been doing. During his time as Mayor, he spearheaded renovation across the city and especially in downtown Knoxville in the Market Square area. He also helped to bring Regal (Rivera) Theater to this part of the city. I will discuss many of his political and philanthropic accomplishments later, but suffice to say he was an excellent mayor ... even if I do say so myself.

When his second term was nearing its end, Bill decided to run for the office of Governor. We had dealt with the ins and outs of local elections, but this decision took things to another level. One thing you learn in such experiences is that, when a family member runs for major political office, you need to develop thick skin because people are going to say a lot of unkind things about your entire family. Negative, hurtful things were said about me, my sweet wife, Natalie, and other members of our family.

You have let it roll off you like water off a duck's back. To that end, I learned to completely avoid what was being said on social media. I think the anonymity and lack of face-to-face interaction online allow people to say things they would never say to their worst enemies if they were actually looking them in the eye. During a campaign, it is best just to avoid it altogether—and to keep looking people in the eye.

Bill accomplished a tremendous amount of good during his time as Governor. It would take too long to list all of his accomplishments (and he wouldn't be very happy about my doing so), but a few of them are most definitely worth mentioning. Under his leadership, the Tennessee Promise program came into being, which provided free tuition for all Tennesseans to Tennessee community colleges. This literally paved the way for millions of people to access higher education.

However, Bill was also highly involved in improving education at the elementary and secondary levels, which is evidenced by the fact that over $1.5 billion was spent on K–12 education during his time in office. Five hundred million of these dollars went to teacher salaries, and student scores increased dramatically from elementary standardized tests to the ACT college-entrance exam.

However, he was not just focused on increased funding; he was focused more on efficient structure and leadership in higher education. For many years, the University of Tennessee Board of Trustees was made up of a large conglomeration representing many of its member entities. The University of Tennessee has campuses or major programs in Knoxville, Chattanooga, Martin, and Memphis, which meant each of these schools had representation on the board. The board also had one representative from each congressional district. All told, it had become a very large, political, and inefficient governing body.

Secondarily, there were similar problems in the other state-run higher education system in Tennessee: the Tennessee Board of Regents. In addition to thirteen community colleges and twenty-seven technical colleges, the universities that comprised this system included Tennessee State University, Tennessee Technological University, Middle Tennessee State University, East Tennessee State University, Austin Peay State

University, and the University of Memphis. Once again, the Board of Regents was comprised of representatives from each of these organizations, which created many political and logistical logjams in its organization and functioning.

Bill addressed these issues through The FOCUS Act. This act reorganized the University of Tennessee Board of Trustees into a much smaller, more efficient governing body. The act also allowed each four-year university under the Board of Regents system to create and maintain its own university boards instead, granting greater influence and efficiency to each school. The Tennessee Board of Regents now only exists to represent community colleges and technical schools.

Beyond education, Bill Haslam also helped Tennessee take enormous strides from a fiscal standpoint. When he entered office in 2011, the state "rainy day" fund was at $284 million. When he left office in 2019, it had grown to $861 million. In light of the deteriorating infrastructure of Tennessee roads and highways, he also spearheaded the Improve Act, which cut taxes on food and increased taxes on petroleum products. The net result was that Tennesseans paid $500 million less in taxes, while much more money was put into cities and counties to deal with their crumbing infrastructure. By the end of his second term, Tennessee was rated the best state in the country for financial stability.

I could go on forever, but time does not allow it (and neither does Bill).

Get Involved

To summarize our family's story in the political process, we have been fortunate on all sides. There were many candidates whom we supported who did an incredible amount of good in the world—and we were lucky enough to partner with them in the democratic process for which so many have laid down their lives to defend.

I encourage you to do the same. Find people who are willing to offer themselves to the service of others, and then offer them your time, talent, and treasure. We've been so fortunate to work with honorable men like Howard Baker, Fred Thompson, Lamar Alexander, Bill Frist, Don Sundquist, President Ronald Reagan, President George H. W. Bush, President George W. Bush, and yes, my own son, Bill Haslam, for whom we took a more active role than just fundraising.

I encourage everyone to get involved in the political process in some way, even if it's only knocking on doors for a candidate you believe in. I remember knocking on one door in Greeneville, Tennessee, that affected me deeply. A lady answered the door and told me she was not going to vote because she distrusted the political process. I understood her concerns, and we discussed the matter for quite some time.

> I encourage everyone to get involved in the political process in some way, even if it's only knocking on doors for a candidate you believe in.

I guess that something good happened in that conversation, because afterwards, she decided to vote. Lucky for us, she voted for Bill Haslam for Governor. I had given her one of my business cards and, after the election, she called to say that she had not voted in over twenty years, but after our conversation, she had had a change of heart.

It just goes to show that no matter how small it may seem in the moment, what you do or say really does make a difference.

CHAPTER 9

ATHLETICS AND BUSINESS

Extraordinary Teams

Though I have already shared some of the experiences I had in football, I think it would be compelling to share a few more, but to also show you how they have specifically helped me learn to lead teams in business.

The thing about leading by example is that, before you can do it, someone has to do it for you. Put another way, we have to *learn* by example before we can *lead* by example. It will come as no surprise that General Neyland was one of the people in my life who showed me what quality leadership looked like. Of course, I had no idea at the time all the ways I would someday apply his principles to the rest of my life.

I was an average football player who was blessed to play on some fantastic teams. This taught me early on about the importance of surrounding yourself with people more talented than yourself, a lesson that would prove invaluable in business. In the three years I had a starting position at the University of Tennessee, we won twenty-nine games, lost four, and tied one. I was surrounded by incredible players the whole time, so much so that nine out of the twenty-two players on our team went on to play in the NFL, with some becoming standout players even in that competitive field. Three of my teammates are enshrined in the College Football Hall of Fame: Hank Lauricella, Doug Atkins, and John Michels. Doug is also in the Pro Football Hall of Fame, and Hank was the runner-up for the Heisman Trophy in 1951. Additionally, Jack Stroud, Ted Daffer, Andy Kozar, Bert Rechichar, Jimmy Hill, Gordon Polofsky, and Bud Sherrod all played in the NFL. Doug Atkins and Bert Rechichar were both first-round draft picks. Stroud, Atkins, and Rechichar all played in the NFL for over ten years and were Pro Bowlers.

> General Neyland was so passionate about playing and beating the best that it ingrained in me the concept that I had to beat Alabama in order to be successful.

Playing alongside such incredible teammates and having so many unique and shared experiences with them also prepared me for a career in business. Each win and each loss taught me something (even though I always preferred the wins). In fact, while the daily experiences of being on these teams were in themselves very inspirational and instructive, there are three football games in particular that really stick out in my mind in terms of learning the principles and lessons that I have spent the rest of my life applying to business.

University of Alabama (1950)

One of the first concepts I learned from General Neyland and from the experience of playing football was paying attention to who or what you're up against. Since freshmen couldn't play on the varsity squad, they were generally tasked with running the plays of upcoming opponents so that the varsity could practice.

During my first year, we learned so much about preparation and practice through studying our opponents so we could emulate their plays in practice. In particular, I learned that matchups matter ... *a lot.* You can prepare all you want, but if you aren't up to speed on your opponent—whether it is a person, a particular play or scheme, or even the weather conditions or climate—then you are only half-prepared.

Pay attention to what you're up against. That is how you fully prepare.

As freshmen we practiced every day against the varsity, but Thursday practices were always held inside the stadium, which was called Shields-Watkins Field at the time. At the end of practices, General Neyland would always yell, "Big circle!" When we heard him yell, we would come running and assemble in a perfect circle to his liking. He would stand in the middle and begin every talk calling us by what he was actively helping us to become: men.

During the big circle time on the Thursday before we played Alabama, he said, "Men, you haven't lived until you've beaten Alabama." He paused for a second, then continued. "In Birmingham." Back then, when we played Alabama on the road, the game was in Birmingham rather than Tuscaloosa. Auburn played all their big games in Birmingham as well. General Neyland was so passionate about playing and beating the best that it ingrained in me the concept that I *had* to beat Alabama in order to be successful.

Freshmen were not eligible to play back then, so I had to wait until my sophomore year in 1950 to finally take my turn to try to beat Alabama. It was the first really big football game of my college career—and it didn't disappoint. At the time, Shields-Watkins Field held about 50,000 people; there was not an empty seat to be found.

Good thing for all those people that the tickets only cost four dollars.

With four minutes left to go in the game, we were down by a score of 9–7. We had the ball and were driving on them, needing a score to secure a win. During this drive, twice we faced third-down-and-ten situations. We picked up the first down on both of them, running a reverse on one play to Bert Rechichar.

When the game clock was down to about forty seconds, we faced a fourth and goal on the two-yard line. Well-known Tennessee and future NFL player Andy Kozar was our fullback. He took the handoff and dove over the goal line, scoring a touchdown and winning the game. We beat Alabama and, even though it wasn't in Birmingham, I had never felt so alive.

During the game, I sustained a small injury to my wrist and was being attended to in the training room. General Neyland's office was directly next to the training room, and I'll never forget overhearing what he said to one of the sports writers during the post-game interview. The reporter said, "General, at the end of the game today, everyone in the entire stadium was standing and watching to see if your team would win or lose, but you were the calmest person in the whole place—just sitting there calmly in your seat."

If you look at old pictures, then you will notice that coaches didn't generally stand up and pace the sidelines during games like they do today. They usually sat on the bench. General Neyland actually kept a chair on our sideline, and he rarely left it during the game.

The General turned to the reporter and said, "I have meticulously prepared my team for any contingency, so all I can do is sit back and await the outcome." That was General Neyland to a tee. He taught us to painstakingly prepare ourselves while also paying close attention to whatever challenges were ahead of us. We always knew to respect the challenge while maintaining the expectation that you could—and would—conquer it.

There were plenty of summer practices when the temperature would reach the high 90s or 100s. Back then, we weren't given regular water breaks like players are given today; there just wasn't as much education about the importance of hydration. On these extremely hot and difficult days of practice, General Neyland would always say, "Men, it's hotter in Tuscaloosa." This stuck with me because it reminded us all that the path to victory goes through humility, discipline, respect, and, ultimately, adversity.

When we circle up the team that I lead, I often think of these lessons from the General.

University of Texas (1951)

The second big game that comes to mind was against Texas in the 1951 Cotton Bowl. Though the game was played in 1951, it was the post-season game that wrapped up our 1950 season. We were ranked number four, and Texas was ranked number three. I've mentioned earlier in the book that we won the game, but the memories of the game itself are worth sharing.

I don't recall people talking about point spreads very often in those days, but there was no doubt that Texas was favored, especially since the game was being played in Dallas. Before the game, General Neyland wrote down and went over his Game Maxims with us as he always did, but this time, he had some added motivation.

> This stuck with me because it reminded us all that the path to victory goes through humility, discipline, respect, and, ultimately, adversity.

"Men," he said, "this team is bigger than you. They're stronger than you. And they're faster than you." We hung on his every word, hoping that this speech was going somewhere better—and fast. Then he pointed to his chest and said, "But you got it in here. We're going to come back in here at halftime and we'll be behind, but we will win it in the fourth quarter."

He knew how not to just pump us up and convince us we could win; he knew how to help us see our limitations so we could address them realistically and give ourselves the best chance to overcome them. As we went through the tunnel and waited to be called to the field, we could hear the Texas band playing "The Eyes of Texas." The entire stadium—minus a few Tennessee fans—was singing with all their might. The General remained unfazed, turning to us and saying, "Men, at the end of this game, they'll be playing 'The Tennessee Waltz.'"

At halftime, just as the General had predicted, we trailed by a score of 14–7. We made adjustments and kept fighting as hard as we could. Neither team managed to score in the third quarter, but then we scored another touchdown in the fourth quarter to seemingly tie the game. However, our kicker missed the extra point, leaving us down 14–13.

After a strong defensive series, we were able to get the ball back. We drove down the field and scored, putting us up 20–14. However, Texas still had enough time—about a minute—to pull off a game-winning drive. The Texas quarterback dropped back for a pass, but it was intercepted by Jimmy "Cowboy" Hill from Maryville, Tennessee.

Bill Stern was the announcer that day and, when Jimmy intercepted the pass, Bill screamed, "They'll erect a statue for him in Maryville!" We kidded Jimmy about this for the rest of his life—the play that made him famous. Ultimately, General Neyland was right again, and we prevailed by the final score of 20–14. Jimmy was just the right guy who stepped up at just the right time. More on that later.

University of Kentucky (1951)

The third game that really sticks out to me was played against the University of Kentucky in 1951, which, of course, was the year we won it all. Just as it is today, Tennessee and Kentucky always played in November, which meant the seasons would be changing and harsher weather was usually upon us. Every time we played Kentucky, it rained or snowed.

In 1950, we had beaten them in Knoxville by a score of 7–0. Now, in 1951, the weather had taken a bad turn as it snowed and rained the entire game, covering the field in Lexington with snow and mud. Coach Paul "Bear" Bryant's Kentucky team was ranked in the top ten, while we were ranked number one. Two of the greatest defensive minds of the century once again went head-to-head. Under those kinds of conditions, it's no wonder the game was still scoreless at halftime.

We finally scored a touchdown in the third quarter. Kentucky then drove down the field for a first-and-goal situation from the five-yard line. Their quarterback was a superb player named Babe Parilli, who ended up coming in third in the Heisman Trophy voting that year. Ironically, Hank Lauricella, our tailback, came in second. Needless to say, there were some serious heavyweights squaring off in this game, and since Parilli had beaten us when we were freshmen, we aimed never to lose to him again.

We didn't.

Parilli dropped back to pass when he was suddenly tackled by Bill "Pug" Pearman in the backfield. Parilli fumbled the ball and Pug recovered it around the fifteen-yard line. Kentucky was never able to recover, and we went on to win the game 21–0. This was a key win on our way to a national championship.

From Football Maxims to Business Acumen

It was a chance encounter that got me thinking about the connection between General Neyland's maxims and running a team in business. Back when my mother was still alive and living in St. Petersburg, I flew down to Florida to see her. On the trip home, I sat next to an SEC official whom I vaguely knew. We began talking about football and such.

He asked me about my job. When I told him that I owned a chain of gas stations, he said, "Well, I bet you're using what General Neyland taught you in football and making good use of it in business." It was a passing comment that I agreed with in the moment. However, when I got off the plane, I really started thinking about General Neyland's methods for coaching a football team and their direct correlation to managing a business in general—and to Pilot, in particular.

First of all, he recruited the best players. Any quality coach knows that you recruit *players*, not *positions*. Yes, there must be a certain degree of physical talent in order to play at a high level on the football field, but there are also other intangibles that greatly affect a team and its outcomes. These include attitude, leadership ability, motor (that is, one's innate ability to move forward with the right attitude), and tenacity. Without these, many a fine athlete has grossly underachieved.

In football, *muscles* cannot make up for a lack of *moxie*. The same is true in business.

We may own and operate gas stations, convenience stores, and travel centers, but our real business is serving people. For this reason, we do our best to seek out and hire the kinds of team members who will uniquely own the mission of Pilot Company and work *with* us, not *for* us.

> **We may own and operate gas stations, convenience stores, and travel centers, but our real business is serving people.**

Next, General Neyland put the best players in the best position that suited their abilities. Coming out of high school in those days, most guys played both ways: offense and defense. A player could be famous as the best running back in his high school's history, but, in college, his best fit—the one that would elevate both his personal career and the performance of his team—might be as a defensive back. A good coach—and a good leader—will work hard to put team members into the right positions reflective of their abilities. At Pilot Company, we have a motto: "Right Person, Right Place," or as we sometimes call it, "RPRP."

Next, General Neyland would make sure we practiced often and that we practiced the right way. This meant we practiced with intensity, teamwork, and a drive never to settle for where we were, but always push forward towards improvement. This also meant practicing in preparation for that week's game plan, which General Neyland always crafted with intentionality. Finally, he would expect us to put it all together towards a win on Saturday.

All these principles mirror what we do in business. Again, we try to get the best people on our team and put them in the right position. One person might be working in the office at present, but he or she would be better off working at one of our travel centers, or vice versa. We put a lot of time into consistently training our teams, orienting them not just to their respective roles and tasks, but also to the overall game plan for the company. And finally, in the case of Pilot Company, we aren't expected to perform just on Saturdays; we must perform twenty-four hours a day, seven days a week, three hundred and sixty-five days a year.

If you don't have good players, you aren't going to win. If you don't put your players in the right position, you aren't going to win. If you don't practice well, you aren't going to win. If you don't have a game plan, you aren't going to win. Finally, you most certainly won't win if you don't put all of these into place for the purpose of performing well on Saturdays ... or, in the case of business, every day you are open.

As it turns out, the SEC official on that airplane was right: the principles of business really are the same as the principles of football.

The Values of Pilot Company

After doing business for so many years and contemplating General Neyland's maxims and other leadership principles, our company landed on four main values that drive everything we do. Whether it is a matter of what we sell or of moving towards travel centers instead of convenience stores, Pilot has changed many times over the years. However, we are confident that these values will remain the same regardless of our company's need to adjust to the dynamics of a changing market.

Value 1: People

The first thing we must always focus on is the same thing General Neyland focused on: people. I've already mentioned the importance of getting the right people on your team, but this is more about remembering that the people themselves are the most valuable part of the company. They must be treated with respect and care, regardless of the bottom line.

We have a lot of stores in coastal areas such as South Carolina, Texas, and Florida. These areas are constantly being affected by hurricanes that sometimes devastate many of the local businesses, including ours. When a big storm hits, we are sometimes required by the authorities to temporarily close stores affected by the carnage. When this happens, we always continue to pay our team members, even though they can't come to work and the store is not generating any income.

Since we employ over 28,000 team members, there are often other things happening in their lives—situations and crises that provide opportunities for us to care for them well. We've had team members who have lost homes, experienced health problems, or have had to live without power for weeks on end. We have a compassion fund for these kinds of things, but we try to go even further in assisting them.

After one hurricane, we were contemplating how to help a number of our team members who were without power. We considered sending them goodie baskets, but one of our team members recalled a similar experience in his own life. He said that when his life unexpectedly went out of sorts, what he really needed the most was *money.*

So in addition to continuing to pay them until they could return to work, we also added a little extra money to their paychecks just to help them get through the days they would be without power. A few months later, I stopped by one of these stores. One of the ladies working that day approached me and expressed her deepest gratitude for the extra help. They had lost everything in their freezer, so the extra money really helped them stay above water financially.

In business, people must come first—and your team is made up the most important people who will determine the success of your company. We do a special monthly birthday celebration for the Store Support Center team members who have birthdays in that month, giving them a free meal and playing various games for gift cards and prizes (but mostly, just for fun). We also allow them to fill out an anonymous survey in which they can give us their positive and negative feedback on any and all aspects of the company. Our Executive Leadership Team then addresses their concerns at the party. We want them to know that we are not only listening but are also accountable to them since all of us own the welfare of the company together.

Valuing people means taking care of one another, just as General Neyland taught us to take care of each other on the football team. We try to take good care of our people because we know they take good care of the company.

There is no value higher than them.

Value 2: Work Hard

It can't be overstated that there is simply no substitute for hard work. No matter what it is that you do, you have to actually do it if you want to get it done. And if you want it done well, you're going to have to work hard.

I think that having a military leader with war experience as our football coach brought another level of work ethic to our team. General Neyland knew the way you conducted yourself with even the simplest of tasks was a reflection of the quality of the outcome you would achieve. A Saturday game

> How we do all the things we are tasked with—big and small—is a key indicator of our character, as well as our success.

was no more important than a Tuesday practice, even though there would be no trophies handed out after the practice. Working hard on Tuesday when no one but your coaches and teammates were watching, regardless of the task at hand, prepared us to work hard on Saturday when thousands of fans were watching us from the stands. Hard work is not something you can just *turn on* when the task is seemingly more important.

At Pilot, we want to elevate this kind of work ethic and expectation at every level of the organization, from the CEO's office to the first-day team member cleaning a shower at a travel center. How we do all the things we are tasked with—big and small—is a key indicator of our character, as well as our success.

Value 3: Work Together
Business is a team sport. Today's world is obsessed with promoting the star on the ball field or the court—the one who stands out with extraordinary abilities. But take it from a man who played alongside many gifted athletes: not one of them ever singlehandedly won us a game. In football, there are eleven players on the field at the same time. If ten of them do their job well and one of them does not, the whole team will suffer.

Our business operates a chain of nearly seven hundred travel centers, but if one of them performs poorly, it reflects on the whole company. We want our team members to embrace the fact that they are being supported—and counted on—by the rest of the team. We want them to embrace this healthy sense of accountability. It is all too easy to get bogged down or discouraged by a difficult task or a persistent problem in one's own department or role. When we do this, we can forget that others are facing similar circumstances in their roles. Remembering the team causes us to feel less isolated and discouraged because we realize we're not alone.

Of course, the best thing about working together is that, when someone does get bogged down with a problem, there are plenty of other team members there to lend a helping hand. It takes humility to ask for help, but those who never ask for help severely limit their own potential. And in the case of a business, they inadvertently do harm to the company. We desire an environment in which leadership can be confident in each and every team member's ability to fulfill his or her role with excellence, as well as one in which everyone knows they are not expected to perform perfectly by themselves with no help from other team members.

A team filled with stars who can't play with others is toxic to a business!

Value 4: Demand Results

Even though a Tuesday practice was just as important as a Saturday game, the game was most definitely a different level of challenge. Practicing against our teammates was a night-and-day difference from facing our opponents in the game. General Neyland expected us to take everything we had learned during the week and apply it even better during the game.

In business, there are moments when all the training, organizational strategy, and preparation gives way to actually *conducting business*. We can train all day long on how to be kind to customers when they walk through the door of one of our travel centers, but if the person working that day presents a sour face to a customer, the whole company has failed in that one moment. Is that too harsh? No. The fact is, in that encounter, we did not achieve the results we set out to achieve.

A lot of companies start off by demanding results, which produces an environment of unhealthy competition, insecurity, and ultimately, a results-over-people mindset.

A lot of companies start off by demanding results, which produces an environment of unhealthy competition, insecurity, and ultimately, a results-over-people mindset. That's why this value comes after the other three. Demanding results only works when every individual on the team knows he or she is valued and commits to valuing others in return. Demanding results from people who haven't been properly trained to work hard at the task they've been assigned and who don't know how to work together toward a common goal will just end in negativity.

But if we keep these values properly aligned, we can *demand* results from our team members with confidence because we know they *desire* the same results. When people are valued, equipped to work hard, and surrounded by supportive team members, there's a collective desire to take the field and put everything that's been prepared into action. When this happens, the results everyone demands of themselves flow from a positive culture, not just from a list of expectations.

Rick Barnes, the Head Coach of Men's Basketball at the University of Tennessee, is a good friend. He recently came and spoke to about fifty or sixty of our leaders at Pilot Company. Rick spoke about building the kind of culture where everyone can expect and demand the same results that lead to a positive outcome for all who are involved in the process. He said it all begins with the leader being willing to listen to his players because, if he doesn't listen to *them*, they will never really listen to *him*. In the same way, he as the coach has to respect them because again, respect will never come his way if he doesn't extend it to them first.

Coach Barnes said doing this requires him to have humility, something people often mistake for weakness in today's age. Great leaders learn how to maintain complete control of the organizations they lead, but also remain humble as they do it. In the case of being a basketball coach, this means being accountable for the outcome of the entire team. I know General Neyland would have agreed with Coach Barnes. Being accountable as the leader is the key to being able to demand healthy results from your team.

Coach Barnes used the hypothetical example of his team being behind by one point with ten seconds to go in a game. If he calls a play that his team executes with precision, but the play doesn't work and leads to a loss, he is personally accountable for those results. However, if one or more of the players do not execute the play he draws up and they lose, then that's on them.

But no matter who bears the fault, the final result is the same: a loss for the team—and the coach will ultimately be held responsible for a loss more than the team members. Understanding this level of accountability encourages everyone at every level of a team or business to embrace the common values and goals of the team and ultimately demand the same results of himself or herself at all levels.

It works on the field, the court, or in the marketplace. In fact, I believe any person who has been successful in athletics at a high level and who will also choose to apply these same lessons and values to business will ultimately find success. The good news is that the same rings true for those who aren't athletes at all. In other words, you don't have to endure a General Neyland practice to learn from him; you can just listen and apply these principles.

It will be worth it. And the good news is that you can take all the water breaks you want.

CHAPTER 10

COMMUNITY AND PHILANTHROPY

Beginning with Faith

THE TERM COMMUNITY GETS THROWN AROUND A LOT THESE DAYS. IT is a little hard to define because it lies at the intersection of so many other important things. In my case, being involved in our community includes more than just giving time or money to worthwhile endeavors or organizations, though it certainly includes that. Real community is something you are a part of, which means you realize it is helping you and not just the other way around.

For me, this includes being active in serving our church and other faith-based endeavors, serving the university that has meant so much to our family over the years, and involving myself with philanthropic organizations that work with the underprivileged. And again, it also means being involved in the political process so the systems that serve people are constantly being tended and improved—sharpening the axe instead of just swinging it harder.

In this chapter, I want to share about people, stories, and perspectives that intersect all these aspects of community and philanthropy in various ways. Before I jump into this, I want you to know that anything good I have the honor of doing or supporting comes from the fact that I have been blessed by God. In other words, there is nothing good in word, deed, or gift that doesn't originate from God. All that we have is His. Our job is to steward these resources that He has chosen to entrust into our hands in a way that pleases Him. In this way, our strong belief and constant activity in community and philanthropy are just extensions of our faith.

None of us grows in faith or positively affects a community by ourselves. In my family, for instance, many people have helped us grow and find more ways to serve. Throughout the 1960s, 1970s, and 1980s, I had the honor of helping bring four different priests to St. John's. I would like to mention them because they were key threads in the fabric of our faith as a family—and for me as an individual.

> **None of us grows in faith or positively affects a community by ourselves.**

The first Rector I helped bring to St. John's was Frank Cerveny. He and his wife, Emmy, came to Knoxville in 1968 and only stayed about three years, but his impact was profound upon me and my family. He was not only one of the best preachers we have ever heard, but he was also an extremely effective and genuine minister who gave of his time and energy to anyone, in any situation, who was in need. He was so dear to us that when Natalie and I were married, he walked her down the aisle.

The next couple who had such a lasting effect on our lives and faith was Dan Matthews and his wife, Deener. An articulate teacher and wonderful friend, Dan was the priest at St. John's from 1972 through 1980. He has been an integral friend to our family for years. He came to our house the day Cynthia died, which was to be expected because Dan was always there for us in good times and in bad.

I doubt you will find another minister who has been as involved in a family throughout so many seasons of life as Dan. He officiated my wedding to Natalie in February of 1976, as well as Jimmy and Dee's wedding in December of the same year. About ten years ago, he also married Whitney and J.W.—Whitney is our oldest grandchild, the daughter of Jimmy and Dee. Just imagine: Dan has officiated weddings for three generations of the same family! That's how much he has meant to our family over the years. His influence has led me to truly believe in the higher calling of serving others.

The third Rector who impacted our lives at St. John's was Jim Sanders. Jim was a person who had worked in business before entering the ministry. It was actually the tragic bombing in 1963 of an African-American church in Birmingham, Alabama, which killed four precious girls, that inspired Jim to leave the business world and become a priest. His family sacrificed quite a bit so he could train and enter the ministry.

For many people in evangelical circles, the term *Rector* is perhaps unfamiliar. It is derived from the word *director*. Jim Sanders was truly a director who helped our church get into much better shape from an organizational, administrative, and community standpoint. Jim's wife, Sally, was also one of the most trustworthy people we've ever met. All in all, the Sanders served our congregation admirably.

During Jim Sanders's time, our church became a cathedral, which means we are now the mother church of our particular diocese. Because of this change, we now have a *Dean* rather than a Rector. Our current Dean is John Ross. John was a priest at our church under Jim Sanders for ten years, and he has been the Dean for an additional twenty-five years. This speaks to John's faithful service and humble longevity in ministry. It is uncommon for one priest to serve at the same place for thirty-five years, but we are so very grateful that John Ross serves our cathedral.

Our time at St. John's continues to be formational, but over the years, we have also been broadened in our spiritual growth by those *outside* the Episcopal Church, especially through a program called the Ministry of the Laity and a local Bible study.

This broadening began with a pastor named Bill Barron. He was the minister at Sequoyah Hills Presbyterian Church, a community church in a neighborhood by the same name. Since St. John's is our church, the only time we generally attended Sequoyah Hills was to attend weddings and funerals. While it may sound funny, Bill was simply terrific at officiating funerals. After one funeral, I told him to let me know if I could ever do anything for him.

Several years later, Bill took me up on my offer and invited me to lunch. We sat down, and he shared an idea called the Ministry of the Laity. Natalie and I partnered with him to help get the program going, which entailed discipleship training based upon various books of the Bible. The program, which contained about six classes, lasted for over ten years and impacted a lot of people for good.

The final influencer I'd like to mention here is John Wood, pastor of Cedar Springs Presbyterian Church in Knoxville. This is the church that my son Bill, and his wife, Crissy, attend. It is more evangelical than St. John's. This is a great example of the way God can use people from different perspectives to enrich your life and the community around you. We shouldn't all look or think exactly the same. Where would be the fun or depth in that?

Bill Sansom convinced me to join his Bible study. It was in this group that I got to know and respect John. He has spoken into my life many times and in many ways, which has affected the way I see the world and my role in the community.

I've been involved in the church in many different ways, which included serving the leadership in whatever role was needed. Again, so much of serving the community, whether religious or otherwise, is looking at yourself and being honest about what you can do well *and* what you're not at all good at. I wouldn't be the best at teaching a Sunday School class, but I can help in many other ways.

The key for each of us is to learn about ourselves and then get involved where we can make the most impact. Each of these leaders helped me learn more about myself, which made me better prepared to serve others when the opportunity arose.

The University of Tennessee

As I briefly stated, one of the greatest service opportunities of my life came when I was appointed to the University of Tennessee Board of Trustees. Lamar Alexander first appointed me when he was Governor. As his second term expired in 1987, my term as trustee was also nearing its expiration. That's when things got interesting.

> "Haslam," he said, "you know, I've got to fill all of these appointed positions and, for the most part, no one cares about any of them. But when it comes to reappointing you or not, everything is so controversial."

The Governor's race came down to a dogfight between Republican Winfield Dunn and Democrat Ned McWherter. The campaign became extremely heated between the two candidates, turning bitter at times. I knew a thing or two about it because I was serving as Winfield Dunn's Finance Chairman.

I knew Ned McWherter as well; he was a good guy who was a beer distributor. Some of the people from the Dunn campaign used this fact against him to discredit him among the more straight-laced conservatives. It didn't take long for Ned's campaign to point out the obvious: Jim Haslam, Dunn's Finance Chairman, was one of the largest beer retailers in the country! This sort of thing demonstrates the tone of the campaign and, needless to say, it was hectic at times.

Ned McWherter won the election, but there were still feelings of negativity on all sides because of the controversial tone of the campaigns. Three years after Ned took office, my term as a trustee was expiring and there were many people from his camp who did not want him to reappoint me. Governor McWherter called me and asked me to come meet with him in Nashville to discuss the matter.

"Haslam," he said, "you know, I've got to fill all of these appointed positions and, for the most part, no one cares about any of them. But when it comes to reappointing you or not, everything is so controversial."

I couldn't help but laugh since I've never been one who has wanted to live anywhere near controversy, not in the slightest.

Governor McWherter was an old-style politician who liked to call it like he saw it. "But look," he continued, "the people who keep telling me I should reappoint you to the UT board are honestly better people than the people who keep telling me I shouldn't. So I'm going to reappoint you."

This was how I was picked for another term to the University of Tennessee Board of Trustees. Governor McWherter and I remained friends until he died. In fact, one of my favorite political stories involves Ned. When my son Bill ran for Governor, his Democratic opponent was none other than Ned's son Mike McWherter. The Monday before the election, I received a call from Ned who said, "Jim, I just wanted to call and congratulate you."

"Governor," I replied, "the election isn't over until tomorrow."

In his quick-witted way, he fired back, "Jim, the hay's already in the barn." And it was, so to speak. The next day, Bill won the election handily.

I was appointed to the Board of Trustees once by Governor Lamar Alexander, once by Governor Ned McWherter, and twice by Governor Don Sundquist. All told, I was fortunate enough to serve on the board for twenty-seven years, which is a long tenure for that type of position.

Back then, the Governor of Tennessee was the Chairman of the Board. At times during my years in this role, I was honored to serve as the Vice-Chairman. I was involved in many decisions during my tenure on the board and was justly criticized at times (and unjustly criticized at others). Through it all, though, I always tried to do what was best for the university and its future.

It bears repeating that my family wouldn't be where we are today and could never have accomplished everything we've accomplished without the University of Tennessee. Natalie and I could never repay the university in time or money for all it has done for us and for what it means to us.

I worked with many incredible leaders at UT over the years. Dr. Ed Boling and Dr. Joe Johnson were the university Presidents during much of my time on the board. Coach Doug Dickey was the Head Football Coach and then the Athletic Director. Coach Phillip Fulmer was also the Head Football Coach and currently serves as Athletic Director. There are many, many others I could name, but time and space would not allow it.

Each of these leaders and many more join me in a strong love for and loyalty to the university. I know without the University of Tennessee, I wouldn't be in this business or in this position to help others. I wouldn't have my family and my closest friends. Simply put, I wouldn't have the very full and rewarding life that God has blessed me with.

Paying the Rent

I vividly remember the conversation that first got me thinking about my obligation to give back and serve my community. I was a young man who had just gotten started in business when I received a phone call from Max Friedman asking me to meet. In those days, everyone in Knoxville recognized the name Max Friedman. The owner of a jewelry store down on Gay Street, he was highly involved in almost every aspect of the community, serving for many years on the city council and actively engaging in the political process. Around Knoxville during this era, he was a legend.

I was curious why he wanted to speak with me. "Mr. Haslam," he said, "We want you to work in the Community Chest." This is what the United Way was called back then.

"Well, Mr. Friedman," I answered, "I am honored that you're asking me, but I just started this business, and I have three young kids at home."

He thought about what I said for a second, then said, "Mr. Haslam, what kind of business are you in?"

"Well, we have a chain of gas stations," I replied.

"And who do you sell gasoline to?"

"I sell to people here in Knoxville and in any of the towns where we have gas stations." He leaned in, and this time, he didn't call me "mister."

"Son," he said, "you have to pay the rent."

I knew what he meant, and I realized right then and there that he was right. If you're going to be involved in business in a community, then you must also give back to the community. He was the first person who challenged me to give back. In all the decades since then, being involved in the community has been one of my most rewarding passions.

> In all the decades since then, being involved in the community has been one of my most rewarding passions.

I don't want to pat myself on the back, so I won't talk about everything our family and company have done in terms of service, but I will tell you some of the *places* where we have been honored to serve. Some of these worthy endeavors are places where you can begin serving in your own community.

We have been involved with the United Way for more than fifty years since 1968. I guess Mr. Friedman's conversation paid off. I have served as the Campaign Chair, as have Jimmy, Bill, and Dee. This organization has helped countless people and has done immeasurable good, and it has been such an honor to serve alongside its members in the community.

I helped launch another key organization in Knoxville after a conversation with Lamar in Japan. We were there in 1983 courting Japanese businesses to come to Tennessee. Nissan had just opened up its stateside factory and offices, so we were hoping that other companies would follow suit.

On the trip, I was sitting next to the Governor's wife, who went by the nickname *Honey*. Honey asked me if we had a leadership program in Knoxville. I asked her what she meant, and she went on to explain the program concept, which entailed identifying and developing key leaders within the community who had leadership potential, equipping them through the program to be more directly involved in community service and projects.

Bill Sansom then the President of the Chamber of Commerce, was on the trip with us. When we returned to Knoxville, we met with other leaders from the Chamber of Commerce, Junior League, and United Way. Donna Cobble was the President of the Junior League, and Bill Arant was the Campaign Chairman of the United Way. The four of us met to discuss getting this program rolling in our city.

The first class of Leadership Knoxville graduated in 1985, and the program has been up and running ever since. It has flourished under the leadership of Tammy White, just as the United Way has flourished under the leadership of Ben Landers. Like all things, the right people serving in the right positions is the key to long-term success, and long-term success means helping more and more people.

Family Legacy

While this part of the book is about community, a few things about family bear repeating here because true, lasting work in the community cannot be separated from family. The very core of the concept of co-piloting is that any good God allows an individual to accomplish in this life can never be accomplished or sustained alone. But let me take it even deeper than this: the essence and longevity of one's legacy is produced by the character and actions of one's family.

To that end, the members of our family have created a legacy beyond what I could ever deserve.

Since much of this story has revolved around the history of Pilot and some of our experiences in politics, you have heard a lot about my two sons, Jimmy and Bill. However, even though my daughter, Ann, has never worked for Pilot or run for public office, she has been just as instrumental in creating and expanding the legacy of our family. Ann is my only daughter and it was evident on the day she entered this world that she is a special person. We have a wonderful relationship that is completely unique. She calls me every single day, which is one of my favorite parts of the day. She is also an incredible wife to Steve and stepmother to Steve's children. I could not be more proud of the leader, wife, mother, and person that she has become—and I couldn't say enough about her if I wrote a hundred books.

In the same vein, Ann's husband, Steve, has also never worked for Pilot, but has been instrumental in building the legacy of our family. Steve has been a part of our family long before he officially joined our ranks by marrying Ann. He grew up two houses down from us, which meant that he was often in our front yard playing ball with all the kids (including me). He is an honorable man and a great husband to Ann. When she was sick in the hospital with her heart condition, Steve never left her side. When they came home, he nursed her back to health for months to follow. As the founder of Volunteer Lumber Company, a company that has grown into a thriving business in East Tennessee, he is quite the successful businessman and leader. But above all, it has been such a blessing to gain another amazing son in Steve.

Again, the unique story of our extended family predates my marriage to Natalie, which makes our family's history all the more rich. Natalie's daughters have never been "step-daughters" to me. They have always been family to all of us, just as my kids have always been the same to Natalie's family. Natalie is Ann's godmother and I am Carol's godfather. Ann and Jennie have been best friends since they attended Sequoyah School together as children. All around, our families have known and loved one another for more years than I can count. I could not be more proud or grateful to have Jennie, Carol, and Susan, along with their husbands and families, as deeply beloved members of our family. We have been enriched by them in ways they will never know.

As far as Jimmy and Bill go, I have bragged on them a bit up to now, but the truth is, much of their successes should be attributed to the fact that God paired them both with spectacular wives. Jimmy's wife, Dee, has been active and successful in business and in many other endeavors, including her work as the Founder and Executive Producer of RIVR Media, overseeing the production of many groundbreaking television shows and movies. She has also been so very active serving the communities of Knoxville and Cleveland, as I will soon describe in greater detail.

Crissy Haslam is also an extremely accomplished and talented person. As you will soon see, her work with children and literacy initiatives is second to none and has changed the lives of countless families. Having watched her for so many years, including the eight when Bill was Mayor of Knoxville and eight more when Bill was Governor of Tennessee, it is so very evident that Crissy is the quintessential First Lady. She exudes compassion, excellence, and class in everything she does. I couldn't be prouder.

As you can see, the blessing of my family is an overwhelming one. Natalie and I each have three children and their spouses (for a total of eleven), who make up the second generation of our family. Their children, along with their own spouses and kids, have created a third generation that consists of twenty-three family members. It keeps getting better as the family has grown into the fourth generation with nineteen great-grandchildren. And at the time of this writing, two family members are pregnant, so the legacy is expanding as we speak.

For a man to whom family is the most important thing in life next to his faith, this family makes me truly rich beyond measure. While I love Pilot, my community, and my university, and I am grateful for how lucky I've been in business, these people—my family—are the real jackpot of my life. I love them dearly and am so proud of each and every one of them.

One of my personal goals was that serving the community would become a family affair. This isn't about titles and positions, and it's not just about donating money. If we have the means, writing a check can be the easiest thing to do. You hand off your money and go on your way. Serving the community and worthwhile causes is about so much more than just finances. If we really want to show that we care and make a significant difference, then we must also give our time and energy. No amount of money can replace the time spent working for worthy causes.

This has become a principle our entire family believes in, and I couldn't feel prouder watching those I love the most roll up their sleeves and get involved in the community. My wife, Natalie, was the first woman to become Chairman of the Board for the Knoxville Symphony and the East Tennessee Foundation. She has also been Chairman of the Board for the East Tennessee Historical Society and active in many other civic activities.

In 1995, Natalie was awarded the prestigious national Amy Angell Collier Montague Medal from The Garden Club of America. This award recognized her ongoing leadership and service in the areas of the arts, education, history, mental health, gardening, and conservation in Knoxville and across Tennessee. In 2017, she was named Knoxvillian of the Year by the East TN Community Design Center and, a year later, East Tennessean of the Year by the East Tennessee Historical Society. She has also been highly involved in service to the University of Tennessee, especially in the College of Arts and Sciences. She has been on the boards of Maryville College, The Webb School, Tennessee Arts Commission, Blount Mansion, Zoo Knoxville, Tennessee Humanities Commission, and the Junior League.

The truth is, my family as a whole has continued to find creative ways to serve each of their own communities with their time, talent, and treasure. Though they don't always like it when I dote on them in public, I would like for you to see just a few of the things they are doing so that you might be motivated to find ways to serve worthy causes in your community as well.

My son Jimmy and his wife, Dee:

+ Have both served as Campaign Chairs for the United Way in Knoxville.
+ Dee also serves on the board of the Emerald Youth Foundation.
+ Both helped fund the Haslam-Sansom Sports Complex in the Lonsdale Community of Knoxville, as well as the Emerald Academy, the first charter school in Knoxville.
+ Dee has also been the Chairman of the Board for East Tennessee Children's Hospital.
+ Jimmy and Dee have both served as Chairman of the Board for Lakeshore Park.
+ Dee has also served on the Advisory Board for the Haslam College of Business, and they have funded numerous programs within the college.
+ Because of their ownership of the Cleveland Browns, they have picked up the same philanthropic torch in Cleveland.
+ They have been involved in funding expansions for Breakthrough Schools and serve with the United Way, Greater Cleveland Partnership, and Rock and Roll Hall of Fame.
+ Dee also serves as the Vice-Chairman of the Board for University Hospital System.
+ They have also contributed to and helped advance education and research through the Disney in Schools Program, as well as aorta research at the Cleveland Clinic.
+ Beyond this, the Browns Foundation has started a program in partnership with the Ohio Department of Education to fight chronic absenteeism in Cleveland-based high schools. The foundation has also helped fund the construction of athletic fields at ten local high schools.

My son Bill and his wife, Crissy:

+ Before their political involvement, my son Bill and his wife,
  Crissy, were always highly involved in philanthropy in Knoxville.
+ Bill was Chairman of the United Way.
+ Crissy worked with Joe Johnson to launch Dolly Parton's
  Imagination Library, a literacy program for children, where
  Crissy also served on the board.
+ Crissy also served on the boards of the Beck Cultural Center,
  the Knoxville Symphony Orchestra, the Arts and Culture
  Alliance, the Salvation Army, and Tennessee Kids Belong, an
  organization that assists families in the process of adoption.
+ Crissy now serves on the board for the University of Tennessee
  Medical Center. Crissy is involved in many endeavors, but it is
  obvious that her greatest passion is helping children, especially
  in the areas of health, education, and literacy.
+ Bill is still extremely active in serving others as well, currently
  serving as the national Chairman of the Board for Young Life.
+ He is also on the board of the Urban Institute, a Washington,
  D.C.-based think tank that carries out economic and social
  policy research to "open minds, shape decisions, and offer solutions," and Teach For America, among others.

My daughter, Ann, and her wonderful husband, Steve:

+ Have focused their energies to serve and give back in the areas of
  church and the arts.
+ Ann serves in numerous roles at our church, including as Senior
  Warden, the highest lay ministry position.
+ She also continues to focus on leading benevolence efforts at
  St. John's. Ann has also been active in the Knoxville Garden
  Club, the University of Tennessee Gardens, and numerous other

activities related to arts and culture in the Knoxville area and surrounding communities.

- Steve is active at church as well, also serving as Senior Warden.
- He has served as Chairman of the Board of the Knoxville Museum of Art and Chairman of the Tennessee Arts Commission.
- He is also on the board for the Cleveland Museum of Art and has been Chairman of the Knoxville Boy Scouts Annual Fundraising campaign.
- In 2014, Steve and Ann also made a transformational donation to the Knoxville Museum of Art that will impact this community for countless years to come, commissioning world-renowned artist Richard Jolley's glass sculpture, *Cycle of Life: Within the Power of Dreams and the Wonder of Infinity*. This work of art is like nothing else, a monumentally scaled sculpture that will remain on permanent display in the Ann and Steve Bailey Hall of the museum. Crafted from thousands of individual cast and blown-glass elements, the larger-than-life sculpture extends more than one hundred feet in length and twelve feet in height, making it one of the largest figurative glass-and-steel assemblages in the world.

Natalie's daughters—Jennie, Susan, and Carol—along with their families:

- Have also been highly involved in philanthropy in the various communities in which they live.
- Jennie, her oldest daughter, and Jennie's husband, Rob McCabe, have been involved in philanthropic endeavors in the Nashville area.
- Jennie has served on the boards of the Girl Scouts and Frist Art Museum.

- She has also chaired fundraisers for the Cheekwood Botanical Gardens, The Hermitage (the home of President Andrew Jackson), the Junior League's Decorator Showhouse, and Cumberland Heights, Tennessee's foremost alcohol and drug addiction treatment center.
- Jennie has also spearheaded fundraising efforts for Harpeth Hall and Ensworth School, which both their children attended.
- Rob has served as the Chairman of the Board for the Nashville Chamber of Commerce, Nashville Downtown Partnership, the Nashville Symphony, Ensworth School, and the Middle Tennessee Boy Scouts Council.
- Susan and her husband, Chip, are active in their community of Marblehead, Massachusetts, just outside of Boston.
- They both serve in their church, Old North Church, and Susan has chaired the Women's Fund of Essex County, which raises money to help local women in need.
- She has also served on the board of the Peabody Essex Museum.
- Chip has served as the Chairman of the Board for Tower Schools and has remained active at his alma mater, Choate Rosemary Hall.
- He also serves the organization known as Squash Busters, which serves underprivileged young men and women, helping them earn athletic scholarships to certain private colleges.
- Carol lives in Vail, Colorado, with her two teenaged sons. Most of her volunteer work has revolved around the outdoors and her sons' activities.
- She has been involved with the Salvation Army, as well as the Colorado Ski Museum.
- She has also raised money for Vail Mountain School and the Ski and Snow Board Association of Vail.
- Carol has also been involved with a number of causes to help animals.

We have loved watching our children serve the community, but these days, we are also watching our grandchildren get involved in many of the same things. That has truly been one of the more rewarding experiences of our lives.

Finding Common Good among Uncommon Goals

Anyone who has seriously served in leadership within the community knows it is not always a bed of roses. I learned a lot about this through my experiences on the Public Building Authority of Knoxville—and I think a few perspectives are worth sharing here.

Knoxville has never had a metropolitan government. We've explored doing so several times over the years, but it has never happened. This means there is no single organization or system that manages the sometimes-conflicting interests of the City of Knoxville and Knox County. As there was growth both in the city and the county in the mid- to late-1970s, it became apparent that some cooperation would help relieve some of the issues that constantly arose. Furthermore, the old City Hall was in disarray after a fire broke out there.

The Chamber of Commerce came up with the idea of housing the city and county governments in the same building, aptly named the Knoxville City-County Building. The powers that be appointed a board called the Public Building Authority to supervise the project, and I was named its Chairman. It was my first experience exercising leadership over diverse groups of people in the same community.

As Chairman of the Chamber of Commerce, I had led a common constituency of business leaders, and it was easy to get everyone on board for something that made "business sense." When I led the United Way, people got behind me because we were serving a common cause. At The Webb School or the University of Tennessee, everyone had the common interest of their children's education in mind—after all, if they didn't believe in the schools, they wouldn't go there or send their kids there. The same was true of St. John's Cathedral—everyone we were working with was there because they shared a common faith and a common belief in doing the good things that naturally flow from it. You didn't have to convince people to change; they were already there because they all wanted the same things as their fellow members. In terms of raising money, the common constituency made all the difference.

However, when I led the Public Building Authority, the mission was to get the city council and the county commission, along with a host of other committees, to come together for a common goal. They had not always played nicely together, so getting them to work together was a challenge. This was a great lesson for me regarding how to lead people of differing opinions to find common ground.

Howard Baker knew how to bring bitter rivals to the table on important issues. He said that no matter what the issue may be, there is always something both sides have in common; you just have to find it and then build upon it. He also said that the key to doing this was never to take credit for any gains that are made. Let the two sides *both* take credit for their work done together. I have always tried to follow his example of leadership.

In serving the community through the Public Building Authority, I learned that people *can* work together, even if they don't necessarily want to. A good leader will help them find their common ground and then help them take single steps on this small acreage until more ground appears at the next stage of the process. Eventually, we were successful and the City-County Building still stands today.

Others' Wisdom on Life and Philanthropy

Natalie gently teases me when I'm asked to speak at events or fundraisers because I usually don't prepare a full speech. Instead, I simply take a stack of notecards upon which are written many of my favorite quotes by authors and leaders who have influenced my life.

As we conclude this chapter on community and philanthropy, I'd like to do the same with you—well, minus the notecards. I find that many wise people have gone before us who can still teach us so much about what it means to serve others well with your time, your talent, and your treasure.

We begin with Dr. Karl Menninger, the renowned psychiatrist. He said, "When you give, you help yourself." We have found this wisdom to ring true in every part of life. When Mr. Friedman challenged me to get involved in giving back to the community, I hesitated because my life was already so hectic. Little did I know how much helping others would energize me. Truly, the only way to feel what I'm describing is to try it for yourself. This is a value that we have tried to pass down to our family not because we are expected to give, but because we know that giving blesses the giver more than the receiver.

Let the two sides both take credit for their work done together.

Alexis de Tocqueville was a French aristocrat who spent a lot of time in the United States in the early 1830s and wrote extensively about his observations of our nation and culture. He said, "I have seen Americans making great and sincere sacrifices for the key common good and a hundred times I have noticed that, when needs be, they almost always gave each other faithful support." His more famous quote was: "America is great because she is good, and if America ever ceases to be good, she will cease to be great."

His basic point here is both simple and profound: he took note that people in America at that time tended to help one another. For him, there was something foundational to our national identity regarding our willingness to lend a helping hand to those around us. Obviously, the country had a long way to go back then—and still does—in terms of equality and equal rights. Even so, we can learn so much from our past, especially when we strive to apply these same principles of goodwill and generosity in a spirit of equality to everyone in our communities. It is this kind of goodness that creates room for our collective greatness.

I heard that David Rubenstein, one of the world's great philan-thropists, said, "Philanthropy is an ancient Greek word that means *loving humanity.* You will certainly think much more of what you have on this earth if you give back." I couldn't agree more. We have tended to relegate the term solely to raising money, but philanthropy does not mean rich people writing checks. After all, not everyone has money to give, but everyone does have *something* to give, including time, energy, and ideas. And certainly, everyone can love his or her fellow man.

Among entrepreneurs, Henry Ford was second to none. He said, "Whether you think you can, or you think you can't—you're right." This one really speaks to the fact that I truly believe optimism is the general dispo-sition of people who are successful and, more importantly, who find ways to help others. Why do they have a better time of it than pessimists? I think it is because they actually enjoy life, not seeing every action or interaction as a means to an end. How you see the world will determine the way you walk in it. I say do your best to focus on the light rather than the shadows.

> And, if you're a good leader, that somewhere will be a better place for everyone who is walking alongside you.

Mother Teresa knew a thing or two about taking action with one's good intentions, but she also knew the power of words. She said, "Kind words can be short and easy to speak, but their echoes are truly endless." It is all too easy to think of helping only in terms of raising money or doing something tangible for people—and these are certainly important. However, never overlook how much good you can do through kind words. This is one of the most important acts of service that anyone is qualified to perform at any time.

Teddy Roosevelt overcame a lot of physical ailments in his child-hood. He was always considered to be a fairly puny, sickly child. Yet he grew up to become an avid outdoorsman, adventurer, soldier, athlete, and leader. He said, "Do what you can, with what you have, where you are." We often wait for perfect circumstances before we try something new or something we know needs to get done. If you wait for perfect circumstances, you'll never do anything. Wherever you are, start there and do the next thing, however small and insignificant it may seem. You can't quantify goodness; it comes equally valued in all sizes.

Ronald Reagan was my favorite U.S. President. There is no doubt that he was also an optimist who saw the world through the lens of potential rather than limitation. He said, "Nothing binds our abilities except our expectations, and, given that, the farthest star is within our reach." When it comes to serving others, it is all too easy to get bogged down in everything that *can't* happen. President Reagan reminds us that our expectations are not static; we have the ability to set them and reset them, whether we realize it or not.

The next one comes from an interesting source; that is, not from a world leader or politician. My friend Lamar Alexander used to quote country music legend Roy Acuff as saying, "Be careful where you aim. You might get there." This goes back to having a game plan and executing it—and the same principles apply to community and philanthropy. The answer is not just *to aim*, but to realize where you *are already aiming* either on purpose or unintentionally and then adjust accordingly towards the right goals, attitudes, or endeavors.

John Quincy Adams once said, "If your actions inspire others to dream more, learn more, do more, and become more, you are a leader." It has always been my goal to strive for this kind of leadership—the kind that makes others better, gives them more opportunities, and enriches their lives. Leading is about *them*, not about *me*. Without *them*, leadership is a lonely walk to a lonely destination that may only help one person: yourself.

Franklin Delano Roosevelt summed it up best when he said, "It's a terrible thing to look over your shoulder when you are trying to lead and find no one there." Secondly, FDR couldn't have been more right about making sure leadership involves people going somewhere *with you*. And, if you're a good leader, that somewhere will be a better place for everyone who is walking alongside you.

Finally, I want to close this chapter with a quote of my own: "Be optimistic, keep things simple, and have a passion for what you are doing."

CHAPTER 11

PILOTING THE HIGHS AND LOWS

Life Stories

I HAVE ALREADY SHARED MUCH ABOUT THE HISTORY OF PILOT Company, but there are so many more stories that have nothing to do with expanding the company, partnering with investors, or changing our methods and models to continue growing in a changing world. Some of our favorite memories are just random stories of day-to-day life as Pilot became what it is today.

Not all of these memories are good. We've had a lot of good things happen to our company, but we've also had our share of bad things. As General Neyland's first two maxims say:

1. *The team that makes the fewest mistakes wins.*
2. *Play for and make the breaks. When one comes your way, SCORE.*

I've tried to point out many of the breaks that, fortunately, the Lord has given me in my life. And, of course, I've tried to make the fewest mistakes possible. However, it is the third maxim that has truly helped us in the area of failure and difficulty: *If at first the game—or a break—goes against you, don't slow down or get rattled. Put on more steam.*

This means that when bad things happen—and they most certainly will—we shouldn't get too upset because things are going against us. We should expect trouble and anticipate the best way to respond. This does not mean you should never get upset; it only means that you don't have to stay in a state of anger or discouragement. There are ways to take action that will help you move out of the storm and towards sunnier skies.

I'd like to share some good and bad stories with you—both are important.

Curbs, Checks, Cream, and Closing

Back in the early days of Pilot when we were just selling gas, there weren't many parking spots at our stores because everyone who drove up was generally using the gas pumps. This meant we had to use curbs to separate the driveway from the other areas, thus one of the tasks assigned to our team members was to keep the curbs cleaned and whitewashed at all times.

I will never forget the day I pulled up to a store in Louisville, Kentucky. When I got out of my car, there was one of our team members doing a great job whitewashing the curb. I was pleased to see the work going so well, so I lightheartedly greeted him. "Hey, whatcha doing?"

"Well," he replied, "that *blankety-blank* who owns this *blankety-blank* place is coming up here soon, so I got to *blankety-blank* clean and paint these *blankety-blank* curbs before he shows up!"

The only thing dirtier than the curbs was his mouth. I never told him who I was and just drove off to my next destination. To this day, I still laugh every time I think about him. Though I wish his attitude would have been a bit more positive, I could tell that he was just trying to do his job.

Another story that comes to mind is about a different team member doing his job, perhaps a little better than he had to. Early on, there were no credit cards and the entire company ran on cash. This meant we had to be careful about cashing customers' checks at our local stores. Our policy was to just not do it.

Knoxville's McGhee Tyson Airport is located in a little town just south of the city called Alcoa. I was leaving early one morning when I realized that I had forgotten to take any cash with me for my upcoming trip. We had a store on Alcoa Highway near the airport, so I stopped by there on my way.

It was so early that the night man was there finishing up his shift. I walked into the store and gave him a check for thirty dollars, asking him to cash it.

"We don't take checks," he emphatically replied.

I gently said, "I understand, but I'm Jim Haslam."

To my surprise, he fired back, "Yeah, I know who you are, and I know that you own the company, but my manager said not to take checks."

> To my surprise, he fired back, "Yeah, I know who you are, and I know that you own the company, but my manager said not to take checks."

And guess what? I didn't get any cash from him. What he was doing was executing his job in accordance with his supervisor's instructions—who was I to deter him?

The curb painter didn't know who I was, and the Alcoa nightshift team member knew exactly who I was. But one of my favorite stories is about a team member who was confused about who I was.

When the kids were younger, I would often take them with me on work trips. We built more fun memories than I can count from our time spent crisscrossing the country together. Once, I took Ann with me to Florida, and we were coming through the Sarasota area. In those days when we were only selling gas, the stations were set up in a style we called *island marketers*, which meant they had rows of pumps on either side with a very small store in the middle.

When I visit a store, I always get the manager's name ahead of time so I can connect with him or her, know how their sales are going, and put a face to the name of the people who make this company go. This particular manager had run a gas station for us up in Sevierville, Tennessee, so we had met several times before. He was walking out of the store to head to the bank as Ann and I were walking up.

I called out to him by name, though I won't use it here, "Hey _____, you remember me, don't you?"

He looked at me intently and replied, "Oh yeah, you're the ice cream man!"

I think he was more excited about the arrival of the ice cream man than the arrival of his boss. I don't blame him, I suppose. I love stories like these because they prove what I always want everyone in our company to know: this business is not about me. This is about the 28,000 team members who make Pilot the great company it is today.

> When I walked back out to meet my sons, they were expecting me to return as the conquering hero I had predicted I would be.

There have been times, however, when I have overestimated my abilities as the founder of the company. One story, in particular, reminds me that I am not the answer to every problem.

The year was 1980, and we were getting deeply invested in the travel center business. Bill had recently started working for us, and I set him about the task of finding us more possible locations to add to the first travel center we had opened up in Corbin, Kentucky. He had found a location with good potential in Florida off I-95 near St. Augustine. I was somewhat familiar with the area.

The property was owned by a gentleman whose family owned a lot of hotels and other properties up and down the interstate. Bill began talks with the owner about the property, but they didn't go well. When he returned to Knoxville, he informed me the owner wanted $250,000.

"$250,000?" I protested. "That's ridiculous!"

I knew what the problem was: my son was green in the business world and needed someone to show him how it's done. I told Bill and Jimmy that we were going to Florida together and that I would demonstrate for them the way we handle tough negotiations so that we still come out on top. They agreed and we were off.

When we arrived, I told Jimmy and Bill to wait out in the front office area while I met with the owner. Once we were inside, I went to work doing what I do best.

"This is a good piece of property," he said, "it will make a good place for you to build your travel center."

"Yes," I replied, "I completely agree. So how much do you want for it?"

"$250,000," was his immediate reply. Ah, but I was not some young whippersnapper and would not be pushed around so easily.

"Hmm," I said with a hint of hesitation, "Tell you what, I'll give you $175,000 for it." I had him right where I wanted him.

I waited for his response. Then I waited a bit longer. He never said anything. This was new to me and, quite honestly, it made me nervous that I would lose the deal. So, after what felt like a lifetime, I volunteered, "Okay, how about $200,000?"

It was fair. I had come his way. This was going to work, right? Silence yet again ensued. I would like to say that this back and forth continued for a while, but the truth is, it was all forth and nothing ever came back. Soon, I found myself saying, "Okay, how about $225,000?"

Silence.

Then I started moving up in $5,000 increments—and I kept moving until I was almost back where we started. Finally, the owner broke his deafening silence, "$250,000 or nothing. You're wasting my time." He paused for a second before hitting me with, "You better hurry up before I change my mind."

When I walked back out to meet my sons, they were expecting me to return as the conquering hero I had predicted I would be.

"How did it go?" they asked.

"We got the property."

"Great! How much did you get him down to?"

I hesitated for a second. "Uh, $250,000," I said sheepishly.

They still give me a hard time about it to this day, and it is one of our favorite memories. After all, everything doesn't always go the way you plan it.

When Crisis Struck Pilot Company

The biggest crisis of our company was certainly something that took me completely by surprise. I don't think our story would be complete without this part, but it was serious enough that I had to consult our legal counsel about whether I should tell the tale. It was most definitely one of those moments for which General Neyland tried to prepare us. In short, a big break went against us in a big way.

The date was April 15, 2013—a Monday I will never forget. Natalie and I had just arrived in Hilton Head that morning. One of my favorite things to do is ride my bike, so, after we had eaten lunch at about 2:00 p.m., I went out for a nice, long ride. Before long, I notice a missed call on my phone and stopped to see what was going on. It was from my assistant.

I called her back and she simply said something funny was going on at the office. Since I was going to be out of the office, she had taken her vacation as well, which meant she wasn't there to really ascertain what was happening. All she had heard was that police were at the Pilot headquarters and that no one was available to talk.

After we hung up, I immediately called Jimmy, but he didn't answer. I then called our CFO; he didn't answer either. This was a terrible few hours because I was out of town and had no clue what was happening with all our team members. At about 4:30 p.m., Jimmy finally called me back and this was the first time I heard any details regarding the most difficult event we have ever faced at Pilot.

To sum up the issue as succinctly as possible, the FBI had been investigating a group of Pilot Company sales executives regarding an alleged practice sometimes called *jacking the discount*. We were served with a federal affidavit with more than one hundred pages of indictments charging us with negligence regarding promised rebates offered to trucking companies that had partnered with Pilot as their exclusive fuel provider. The authorities were accusing us of intentionally skimming off the top of these discounts.

At about 11:00 a.m., the FBI raided our Pilot offices and effectively shut us down immediately. When I say they *raided*, I mean everything that comes to mind with such a term. A team of armed officers wearing bulletproof vests came into the main building that housed the department they were investigating.

They made our team members stand against the wall. One of them fainted. It was a very bad series of events. Furthermore, the same thing was happening at all of our remote locations where any of our salespeople were suspected of being involved in the alleged scheme.

I flew back to Knoxville immediately. The next morning, Tuesday, I drove up the hill that leads to our Pilot offices, just as I always had done. Deep down inside, I was concerned that, when I reached the top, I would find that nobody had shown up for work that day. I was relieved to discover that everyone did.

In the meantime, Jimmy assembled a legal team. On Wednesday, they met with our senior team about the matter. That same day, Jimmy made the following public statement:

> *I've read the affidavits. I now understand more clearly the questions the federal investigators are exploring.*
>
> *I maintain that the foundation of this company is built on its integrity and that any willful wrongdoing by any employee of this company at any time is intolerable.*

We will continue to cooperate with the federal investigation and continue our own investigation into these allegations.

I value the relationships we have with our customers, our vendors and our team members across the country and regret that they have to go through this with us, but I trust and believe their faith in this company and its principles has never been misplaced.

This was a short statement, but it began a long and arduous legal process that would unfold over the coming months and years. But on that first week, our team members at Pilot kept showing up and rallying together so we could get through the crisis at hand—a crisis that would get much worse before it got any better. Jimmy's leadership at this time was extraordinary.

> **Our goal was to simply meet with as many team members as possible and let them know everything was going to be okay.**

The affidavit the government released, which contained many damning and questionable things about our company, was public record. This sparked a huge news story across the nation. Everywhere we turned, newspapers and television reporters were talking about us. The company we loved so much was taking some real shots in the media.

We continued meeting with our legal team. We had to take the time to find out what happened and face the legal ramifications. We also wanted to help rally the troops among our team members to keep them from worrying or panicking. Ken Parent, our Chief Operating Officer, and I went out to visit as many of our travel centers as we could. Our goal was to simply meet with as many team members as possible and let them know everything was going to be okay.

Deep down inside, I hoped we were right.

We also immediately assembled an audit team. Paul Pardue our Internal Auditor who had been with Pilot since 1994, worked tirelessly, putting forth an admirable yeoman effort in gathering all the information necessary to help us respond to our customers and the government appropriately. There were also many additional auditors brought in from outside the company to help determine exactly what had happened. Once we began diving into the numbers, things went from bad to worse in a hurry. Simultaneously, we were being sued by various trucking companies that believed they had been affected by the whole ordeal.

Once we had drilled down to the bottom of the matter in question, we found that it involved less than 5 percent of our total business. Jimmy then addressed the media again through the following statement:

Statement from Pilot Flying J[1] CEO Jimmy Haslam
April 22, 2013

Thanks again for coming out today.

I want to continue to keep you informed of current events here at Pilot Flying J.

As was the case last week, as much as I would like to, I will not be able to take questions because of the ongoing federal investigation. I hope I will answer most of your questions in my remarks.

It still appears to us, based on all we know at this time, that this federal investigation is focused on a narrow slice of our business in which rebates on diesel fuel purchases are manually calculated and paid to a relatively small number of our 3,300 trucking company customers.

We are continuing to cooperate appropriately with investigators, but we are determined to understand on our own the questions they are asking and to do everything we can to make sure we are never in this position again.

To that end, I'm announcing today five steps that we are taking to address the issues raised by the investigation. I'm going to take them one by one.

---

1 Note that we were still Pilot Flying J at this point. The new corporate name Pilot Company was not created until 2020.

1) *Immediately, we are bringing our field audit team to Knoxville to review all 3,300 contracts with our trucking company customers, not just the relatively few implied in the federal affidavit, and to proactively address any miscalculations that we may find.*

Our goal is to understand the entirety of that part of our business, not just the manually processed contracts. If we find an underpayment, we will encourage the affected customer to review our finding, test with their own audit if they like, and, if we owe them money, we will write them a check immediately.

We will be communicating this plan directly to our trucking company customers and moving through this process as quickly as possible. I hope this process won't take more than four to eight weeks, but the important thing is that we get it right.

I've already spoken personally to several of our customers, including Curt Morehouse with Morehouse Trucking and Tommy Hodges with Titan. We are working with Curt to reconcile his account, and I will be going to see Tommy on Wednesday.

2) *Yesterday, we placed on administrative leave several members of our diesel fuel sales team and, on an interim basis, we are restructuring that team pending further investigation to get control of that operation and restore confidence to our customers.*

Placing members of our team on leave is very painful. For years, we have been a trusting, proud family here at Pilot Flying J focused on providing honest, forthright services to our customers. We have had relatively few personnel issues, but we cannot ignore the content of the federal affidavit released last Thursday evening.

We are not judging the guilt or innocence of the team members placed on administrative leave. We are addressing actions and words that fail to show proper respect to our customers and that violate the character, values and principles that have been core to this company since it was founded fifty-four years ago.

As a private company, we have dealt with these members privately and will not release their names publicly.

I have directed that all of our diesel fuel customers be converted to electronic calculation and payment eliminating future risks of any abuse that might be enabled by manual calculation and payment.

This process will fully eliminate manual processing at Pilot Flying J and place all of our customers on electronic direct bill.

I expect this process to be completed by June 30.

3) I have asked our outside counsel to help us create and staff the position of Chief Compliance Officer to report to the company's general counsel to deal with any similar questions or issues that might come up in the future.

The establishment of the position of Chief Compliance Officer is important because, had we had one before, perhaps some team member would have raised a question about manual rebates internally before anyone would ever have gone to federal investigators.

If we had discovered any irregularities on our own, we would have fixed them on our own. That would have been good business, and it would have been the Pilot Flying J way—always do what is right first.

I expect this person to be on the job within thirty days.

4) Lastly but very importantly, our board, in a special meeting yesterday, voted to hire an Independent Special Investigator to report to the board and oversee and validate all of our internal inquiries related to the federal investigation.

Because there is a federal investigation now, we have to take extraordinary steps to do whatever is necessary to repair any damage done to this company's reputation and restore the full integrity on which this company was built.

We will find the best person in America to come into this situation and oversee and make certain that any and all of our own investigations into these matters are thorough and correct and help us ensure that what happened to this company last week never happens again.

I expect this person to be on the job within thirty days.

We know this process is going to be difficult and will probably last for a while, but we are not going to sit by idly in the meantime. We are going to diligently and aggressively figure out for ourselves what's going on, and if we find anything amiss, we are going to make it straight right away.

In closing, we have received tons of expressions of support from our friends here in Knoxville and Cleveland, our customers, our suppliers, and our vendors, and I cannot tell you how much that means to our family and our team members at Pilot Flying J.

Last week was very tough, and it's not over, but we are back to business as usual, we are dealing aggressively with this situation, and we all believe we will come out of this adversity stronger than ever as individuals and as a company.

Thank you very much.

I am proud of the way Jimmy conducted himself and the way he represented our company during such a difficult ordeal. Our board eventually hired Reed Weingarten from the Washington firm of Steptoe and Johnson, who was tasked with initiating his own investigation and then reporting back to our board. Our attorneys also hired an outside accounting firm, Kraft and Company, to engage in a separate accounting process.

On October 14, we settled the class-action lawsuit brought against us by various trucking companies. They had engaged their own accounting firm: Horne LLP. We paid all the trucking companies back what they had been shorted, plus 6 percent interest. We also restructured the entire sales department of the company by redistributing most of the sales team and hiring a new department head.

The legal process continued for quite some time. In October 2014, we finally settled an agreement with the Justice Department, pleading guilty to all the charges. We agreed to pay a $92 million fine. After this agreement, the government held that Pilot Flying J had settled the matter in terms of our company's legal obligations. All told, nineteen PFJ team members and staffers admitted to participating in the scheme. Fourteen pled guilty, three were convicted, and two were found not guilty. The three who were convicted are still appealing their sentences.

Obviously, I was distressed with all that happened during this time, but I was amazed by the way our team members didn't allow the difficulty to keep them down. They kept coming to work—kept laboring alongside us to put the negativity in our rearview mirror and better practices ahead of us. When the dust settled, there were five main lessons we learned from this difficult experience:

1. We had too much autonomy in the sales department of the company. We didn't have complete control.
2. We found that there was a fear within the company of speaking out, which is completely unacceptable. Everything in our culture must be built on integrity, honesty, and accountability.
3. Much of what went wrong was because we didn't have everything in writing. This created too much room for too many bad things to happen.
4. We had an inadequate auditing process, which we immediately changed.

5. We didn't have a complete compliance system within the company.

Since that time, we have done a lot of hard work to remedy each of these issues. On a scale of one to ten in these particular areas (and no company ever runs at a ten, in my opinion), I think that we are running close to a nine now. Our customer base has increased tremendously since the incident, and we have become a better company overall.

Now when I come up that hill to go to work, I often say to myself, "If at first a break goes against you, don't slow down, don't get rattled, and put on more steam." I can tell you that our entire Pilot team stood determined to not be rattled—and they put on more steam. It was not the path I would have chosen, but I know beyond a shadow of a doubt that we are a much better company because of it.

When it all started in 2013, we had five hundred and fifteen travel centers. Today we have six hundred and sixty-eight, our profit has increased by 50 percent, and Pilot Company is selling more than eleven billion gallons a year, including PFJ Energy. All this is a reflection of the hard work of our 28,000 devoted Pilot Company team members under the leadership of Jimmy Haslam and his senior team.

A Final Thought on the Right Team

I would be remiss not to mention some of the most important people who have helped us get to where we are today: our Pilot Company Board of Directors. All companies must have a board of directors that is tasked with a list of fiduciary duties the board must perform. Early on, since we were a small family-owned business, our original board consisted of Bob Campbell, Cynthia, and myself. Together, we conducted the basic affairs of the board. However, as our company grew and things began to change, the composition of the board changed as well—and in ways that would greatly impact our future.

From 1965 through 1988, since Marathon owned half of Pilot, three Marathon Directors came onto our board to join the three we already had. When Cynthia died, Jimmy took her place in 1975, while Bill came onto the board in 1980 after he graduated from college. Because Marathon was an integrated oil company with many people skilled in multiple areas such as marketing, purchasing, financing, construction, retailing, and the like, they were able to lend a wide range of expertise to our board. So when we bought out Marathon (the first time) in 1988, it became apparent that we needed to add more board members who possessed a wider range of skills than Jimmy, Bill, or I could offer on our own.

Our first choice was Jimmy Smith. Jimmy had been the CEO of a large bank and possessed tremendous financial experience. When Lamar Alexander's term as Governor ended, he became the President of the University of Tennessee and was

> It was not the path I would have chosen, but I know beyond a shadow of a doubt that we are a better company because of it.

also a natural choice to come onto the board. Since we had just started in the food business, we also asked Sandy Beall, the founder and CEO of Ruby Tuesday, to join. Then in 1989, Lamar became the Secretary of Education under George H.W. Bush, so we filled his seat with Brad Martin. We had known Brad through politics, and he had also become involved in retail business when he purchased the Proffit's chain of stores in East Tennessee. Eventually, Brad would become the CEO of Saks. In 1995, we also added John McKinnon, the Dean of the business school at Wake Forest. Prior to becoming Dean, John had been the President and COO of Sara Lee.

These four people—Jimmy, Sandy, Brad, and John—were extremely helpful to us in this crucial time of our development. We had quarterly board meetings, usually held at Blackberry Farm. The night before the meetings, we would always bring in interesting people to speak to us, including the legendary UT Women's Baskeball Coach Pat Summit; Cal Turner, the CEO of Dollar General; and Hugh McColl, the CEO of Nations Bank (later Bank of America).

The insight and direction that resulted from these meetings were highly instrumental to the growth and advancement of our company. We were evolving from a company that mainly sold gas and diesel fuel into an interstate marketer. Brad and Sandy's knowledge of the food and retail industries, coupled with John and Jimmy's knowledge of business and finance, were irreplaceably vital to us at this time.

When Marathon once again invested in Pilot in 2001, we added members of their senior staff to the board, including CEO Gary Heminger, Tony Kenney, who ran Speedway's retail operations, CFO Gary Pfieffer, and Rod Nichols, their head of human resources. Then in 2008 when we bought them out again, the private equity company CVC became a stockholder, which meant we added Chris Stadler, Gijsbert Vuursteen, and Gero Wittemann from their company. In 2010, after we completed the Flying J purchase and subsequently bought out CVC, we added Crystal and Chuck Maggelet to represent Flying J.

That same year, because of his friendship with Brad Martin, we were extremely fortunate to convince Fred Smith, the founder and CEO of FedEx, to join the board. He is an outstanding businessman who understands the intricacies of global transportation on a very high level. He agreed to come on for three years, but because of the federal investigation, he remained for five years, providing invaluable direction and insight through many important and difficult seasons. Around the same time, we also added Lee Scott, who had just retired as the CEO of Walmart. The knowledge Lee had gained during his time leading the world's biggest retailer rendered him as one of the most insightful members our team had ever known, helping us see clearly what we were doing and how we could improve. In addition, Lee's humor spiced up our board meetings.

When Fred came off the board in 2015, he was replaced by Rob Carter, the Chief Information Officer at FedEx. Rob has since been instrumental in helping Pilot becoming a better technology company. In 2016, Whitney Haslam Johnson, Jimmy and Dee's daughter and my granddaughter, became the fourth Haslam to serve on the board. We also added Doug Lawler, CEO of Chesapeake Energy. After the Berkshire Hathaway deal, Mark Hamburg, their CFO, and Kevin Clayton, CEO of Clayton Homes, also came on board to represent Berkshire. Consequently, Bill came off the board in 2001 when he was elected Mayor of Knoxville, but he returned to the board in 2019 after leaving the Governor's office.

In a public company, a board has tremendous fiduciary responsibilities, so a large portion of its time is consumed doing so. But in a private company like ours, the board can devote almost all its time to the process of helping the management of the company. This has been the case with the Pilot Board of Directors. Our company could never be what it is today without these individuals, their skill, and their willingness to help us grow and improve. I especially want to mention the contributions of Brad Martin, who, if we were a public company, would be our Lead Director. During the investigation, Brad headed up a special committee of the board that was so valuable in determining what had actually happened and what steps we needed to take to ensure that it never happened again.

Regardless, each of these Directors has contributed to the advancement of Pilot Company in immeasurable and meaningful ways.

What Remains

Highs and lows are a part of life; you can't have one without the other. In fact, both are important to becoming the person you should be, not just the person that you are. As we come to the end of me telling of our story (some of my friends and family still have their own perspectives to share), I'd like to revisit a few values I think are most important. I've already discussed most of these in varying detail in my twelve maxims, but I thought it might be helpful to extract and restate several of these princples here at the end of my part of the story. When the highs and lows come and go like rain—sometimes light and refreshing and sometimes flooding everything—these are some of the principles that remain and can never be washed away.

In the end, integrity must rule the day—or better said, it must rule *every day.* Always try to do the right thing, even when it is difficult. No, *especially* when it is difficult. And if you make a mistake here, go back and make it right at all costs. Your integrity will outlast your success, so make sure you keep integrity first.

> Your integrity will outlast your success, so make sure you keep integrity first.

Work hard and work smart. Do both. Work ethic is one of the surest indicators of success, so learn to put in a full day's effort every day, regardless of whether your boss is watching. However, don't just work at what you're doing without evaluating whether your effort is being expended wisely. Good leaders stay busy doing *what* they are doing while also evaluating the *way* they are doing it. This allows them to maximize the results of their efforts.

As you live your life doing whatever it is you do, it is imperative to *respect everyone you come into contact with.* It is easy to say we should just be nice to people, but if we feign kindness just so things will go easier for us, we are only manipulating people. It is hard to genuinely be kind to someone when you don't actually respect them. So choose to respect them, regardless of whether you think they deserve it or not. Respecting people who have different opinions than you is a key to not just *appearing* to be the person you want to be but also actually *being* that person.

Learning to **lead by example** is a lifelong quest that I am still on. I certainly have not arrived, and I have so much left to learn. But here's the thing: if I don't learn to listen, then I'm not really learning at all. Listening skills are life skills. If you want to learn and be a leader who is an example to others, you must first listen to others.

As I have already discussed, **humility is the disposition of great leaders**. If you want to lead in a way that lasts, you must not demand the head chair, the corner office, or the highest paycheck. You must learn to put others first—that is the key to not only *becoming* a good leader but also *enjoying* it.

Good leaders don't run from accountability; they seek it out. It is all too easy to want to avoid criticism at all costs. Criticism hurts. But when we avoid criticism, we also avoid the feedback that can help us learn and grow. In your family and in business, whatever your family situation or business may be, you must be accountable for your actions and hold others accountable for theirs. It hurts a little when you fall a few inches into the safety net of accountability. It hurts a lot more when there is no net to break your fall.

This also means setting high standards and holding yourself to them. General Neyland's Game Maxims were lofty standards that dictated not how *a practice or game would go* (after all, you can never predict these), but rather how *we would go* no matter what was happening around us. If you don't set standards beforehand, you will not just magically find and adhere to them in moments of stress or success. Decide now what is important in life. Write these things down. Discuss them with your family or team, then take action and gauge your reactions according to these things and not according to the ways you might feel in the moments to come. Feelings are not reliable; standards never change.

This will cause you to be able to set high goals for yourself, your family, and your team. Whatever it is you are doing, why would you settle for mediocrity when you could be pursuing greatness? This is not only a matter of financial success or advancement; it is about allowing your high standards to be the stepping stones for high performance. Set high goals and then be accountable for them.

Have a plan for everything you do. It is rare that someone wanders aimlessly and arrives at a desirable destination. The same is true in life. Your values and standards will help you decide where you want to go, so make a plan and begin taking intentional steps towards an intentional destination.

As you walk, remain optimistic. Again, optimists tend to fare better in this life than pessimists. Pessimists never get anything done beyond the minimum things required of them. They rarely achieve something great and lasting—mainly because they can't see anything great and lasting to pursue. If you always look down, you will always see what's on the ground. But if you look up, you will see everything and there will be no lack of good things to pursue. Don't get discouraged when bad things happen—they are also a part of the path that leads you where you need to go.

> However, you must remember that change is your friend, not your enemy.

Be passionate. Coaches sometimes call this someone's *motor*. Passion is a matter of energy. It flows from the right values and an optimistic attitude. Passion is not measurable, but you can certainly tell when someone has it—and when they don't. If you don't naturally have it, cultivate passion through pursuing the right values of integrity, humility, and accountability. When you believe rightly about what matters most in life, you will find yourself becoming more passionate about continually pursuing these things. If you want to be successful in anything you do, you must be passionate about it.

And finally, embrace change. This is not natural for anyone because change can be scary. However, you must remember that change is your friend, not your enemy. You must continually change or you will be left behind. Again, when faith, family, integrity, and the other values that matter most in life are firmly set as your foundations, then you can feel confident in continuing to embrace change in your circumstances because those things will provide safety for what you build on them. Keep moving to build something—life is not a spectator sport.

I have been blessed with a very full life—and, by God's grace, Natalie and I hope to live many more years. Regardless of the time we have on this earth, I believe these are the things that matter most and that will never fade, even when our bodies do.

How did all of this happen? I'm not completely sure, but it is a question I hope I have at least partly answered in a way that points to the right things. In the end, I have been so very lucky. And it has been the people in my family and the 28,000 Pilot Company team members—my co-pilots—who are my greatest treasure. My story is the story of how they have loved and served me well. I am so eternally grateful for a lifetime in which I can attempt to love and serve them in the countless ways they have done so for me.

I hope you will do the same.

General Robert R. Neyland, legendary Football Coach at the
University of Tennessee and Jim Haslam's mentor.

As an offensive lineman, Haslam wore jersey number 56.

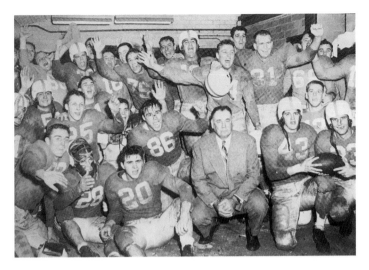

Vols players celebrate around General Neyland after securing
the 1951 National Championship over Texas. Haslam is
wearing a helmet three rows back on the left behind #25.

The 1952 Tennessee Volunteers team photo
featuring Jim Haslam as Team Captain.

After only a few months in Korea and at the age of 23, Haslam was named Company Commander of Headquarters Company, 1169th Combat Engineer Group.

Haslam exiting his tent in Korea.

Haslam with his wife, Cynthia, and their three young children
Ann, Bill, and Jimmy (from left to right). (1960s)

Haslam at his desk in the Pilot corporate offices on Kingston Pike. (1960s)

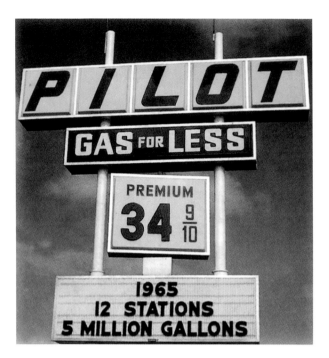

This Pilot gas station sign from 1965 depicts
the size of the company at that time.

Pilot began to evolve in the 1970s and 1980s to offer
more than just gas and cigarettes. (1976)

Jim Haslam married longtime friend Natalie Leach Tucker in 1976. From left to right: Bill Haslam, Jennie Tucker, Ann Haslam, Natalie Haslam, Dan Matthews, Jim Haslam, Carol Tucker, Susan Tucker, and Jimmy Haslam.

Pilot gas station in Knoxville, Tennessee, in 1966.

Pilot's first Travel Center in Corbin, Kentucky, in 1981.

Bill and Jimmy at the Pilot offices. In 1996, Bill became
the President and Jimmy became the CEO.

Haslam at a Pilot pump in the 1980s. After bringing
both of his sons into executive leadership, he was named
and remains Chairman of the Board to this day.

The Haslam family (from left to right): Dee, Jimmy,
Natalie, Jim, Ann, Crissy, and Bill.

Jim Haslam watching as Bill Haslam is sworn in as the
49th Governor of Tennessee on January 15, 2011.

Haslam in the Oval Office (from left to right): Bill Sansom, Jim Haslam, Daryl Akins, Senator Howard Baker, and President Ronald Reagan.

Natalie in red jacket at groundbreaking for the Natalie
Haslam Music Building at the University of Tennessee.

Haslam with football teammates (from left to right):
Hank Lauricella, Jim Haslam, and Andy Kozar.

Haslam with his children (from left to right): Jimmy, Jim, Ann, and Bill.

Jim and Bill at the White House with President George W. Bush.

Peyton Manning presents a check to the Pat Summitt Foundation in 2013. From left to right: Tyler Summitt, Pat Summitt, Peyton Manning, and Jim Haslam.

Jim Haslam and his children (from left to right): Bill, Crissy, Jim, Ann, Steve, Dee, and Jimmy.

Haslam with Natalie's daughters at the presentation of the Horatio Alger Award in Washington, D.C. From left to right: Susan Robie, Jim Haslam, Carol Pattison, and Jennie McCabe.

Thirty-plus members of the extended Haslam family.

Jim with his daughter, Ann Bailey.

Natalie and Jim Haslam.

The current Pilot headquarters is located on Lonas
Drive overlooking I-40 in Knoxville.

At the age of 89, Jim Haslam still goes to work at his office every day.

Warren Buffett's company, Berkshire Hathaway, became a principal investor in Pilot in 2018. From left to right, back row: Dee Haslam, Jimmy Haslam, Dave Arnholt, Steve Bailey, and JW Johnson.
From left to right, front row: Jim Haslam, Natalie Haslam, Warren Buffett, Whitney Johnson, Cynthia Arnholt, and Ann Bailey.

The first Pilot station (store 102) in Gate City, Virginia.

A portrait of Jim Haslam painted in 2007 by John Howard
Sanden hangs in the Pilot corporate offices.

An early Pilot station in Blacksburg, Virginia.

For over sixty years, Pilot Team Members
have served customers with excellence.

Pilot fuel trucks then and now.

Jim and Jimmy Haslam, the CEOs of Pilot Company
from its inception in 1958 to present.

Jim Haslam (top left) coaching Bill's Little League baseball team in 1969. Eleven-year-old Bill is center in the second row.

Pilot Travel Center in Franklin, Kentucky.

An event launching the Tennessee Technology Corridor in 1982. Left to right: Governor Lamar Alexander, President Reagan, Senator Howard Baker, and Jim Haslam.

The signing of the Pilot merger with Flying J in June 2010,
a transformational moment for the company.
Left to right: Crystal Maggalot, Jim Haslam, and Jimmy Haslam.

A painting of Smokey, the unofficial mascot of the University of Tennessee, painted by President George W. Bush as a gift for Jim Haslam.

Hank and Betty Lauricella with Natalie and Jim Haslam.

Former UT Head Football Coach and current Director
of Athletics Phillip Fulmer with Jim Haslam.

Jim Haslam, First Lady Laura Bush, President
George W. Bush, and Natalie Haslam.

Back row: Jimmy Haslam, Dee Haslam, Steve Bailey, Ann Bailey, Chip Robie, Bill Haslam, Crissy Haslam, and Rob McCabe. Front row: Susan Robie, Jim Haslam, Natalie Haslam, Jennie McCabe, and Carol Pattison.

Natalie's daughters, Jennie, Susan, and Carol, at the dedication of the Natalie Haslam Music Building. They are holding the original sheet music for "The Tennessee Waltz," which was presented to Natalie at the event.

Natalie and Jim relaxing.

ACKNOWLEDGEMENTS

It has been my pleasure to tell our family's story and the story of Pilot. Throughout these pages, I have mentioned many friends and family members in detail, though I could never mention them all. To our entire family, all of our friends, the community of Knoxville, fellow parishioners at St. John's Cathedral, and our University of Tennessee family (past, present, and future), I thank you for your constant friendship and encouragement.

Just as neither building our company nor enriching our community just happened out of the blue, neither did the telling of this story. I'd like to thank a few people who have helped us do both.

First of all, many people chipped in on the process of compiling information, writing, editing, proofreading, and a thousand other things to make this book possible. My gratitude begins with my wonderful wife, Natalie, and her truly remarkable skills of editing and proofreading. Also, thanks to my son Bill, who insisted (and kept insisting) that I write this book—he helped bring the right people to the table to make it happen.

A few of these "right" people include my literary agent, Robert Wolgemuth, and the wonderful team at Wolgemuth & Associates, as well as Jonathan Merkh and the excellent team at Forefront Books. All of these have worked so hard to edit and publish this story—and I am grateful. I would also like to thank John Driver, whose exceptional writing skills and engaging personality made writing this book easy and enjoyable. A heartfelt thanks to Bob Kesling, the Voice of the Vols, for lending your wonderful skills to the reading of the audiobook. And finally, thanks to Laura Self, my assistant for the past four years. She makes my life easier while also making me look good—and she has worked tirelessly to help this book (and me) stay on track throughout every phase.

I also would like to extend my sincerest gratitude to our Board of Directors (about whom I've already written), as well as our Senior Leadership Team here at Pilot. Jimmy Haslam, our Chief Executive Officer, has been with Pilot for forty-three years, serving as CEO for last twenty-four. Ken Parent is our President and Chief Operating Officer—he knows Pilot inside and out and is highly respected in the industry. Shameek Konar is the President of PFJ Energy. He has a PhD in Economics from Vanderbilt and understands petroleum supply and distribution at an extremely high level. He will become the CEO of Pilot in 2021.

Mike Rodgers, our Chief Strategy Officer, knows as much about retail technology as anyone in the country. Kevin Wills, our Chief Financial Officer, is a very experienced CFO and has worked for two NY Stock Exchange companies. Jason Nordin is our Chief Operator and carries tremendous responsibility for the operations of our 730 travel centers. Paul Shore is our Chief People Officer—he is a real human resource professional.

Brad Jenkins, who has great commercial skills, works diligently as the Senior Vice President of Supply and Distribution. Kristin Seabrook is Chief Legal Counsel and has held this post with excellence since 2013. David Hughes, our Senior Vice President of Sales, has a keen understanding of the needs of trucking companies. Whitney Haslam Johnson, my granddaughter, is our Chief Experience Officer. She is in charge of the Pilot brand, as well as communications both internal and external. She fulfills these roles in an extraordinary and efficient manner. And Patrick Deptula, our Vice President of Development and Environmental, does a great job of getting projects done on time and on budget. Thanks to these and so many others who work so hard at Pilot to help our millions of customers.

We also have many heartfelt friends who have contributed to our lives, our story, our company, and our community in infinite ways—a special thanks to each of these.

Bill Arant has been involved with Knoxville banking for over forty years. He was President of the Chamber, Chairman of Zoo Knoxville, and United Way Campaign Chair. He is a sports trivia expert and we have enjoyed going to many sporting events and traveling with him and his wife, Barbara.

I have known Hank Bertelkamp since our college days when he was Captain of the Vol basketball team. We have continued our mutual interest in basketball by going to many games together. Hank is a former Chamber of Commerce President and has been generous in the community.

Bill Cobble is a retired Knoxville businessman who loves the Great Smoky Mountains and is an avid conservationist. He has been very active in Friends of the Smokies and is the key person in the revitalization of Tremont. His wife, Donna, was the very first woman to be Campaign Chair for United Way.

When I was Chairman of the Board of the Public Building Authority, Mike Edwards was the Administrator and did a tremendous job. He then became the CEO of the Knoxville Chamber and revitalized the organization. He also became an expert on workforce education.

Sam Furrow, an auctioneer and car dealer, has been an advocate for many good things happening in Knoxville. He has served as Chairman of Leadership Knoxville, Zoo Knoxville, United Way campaign, and many other worthwhile civic endeavors. We have enjoyed traveling to many different places in the United States with Sam and his wife, Ann.

Retired orthopedic surgeon Dr. Frank Gray, who is a man of many talents, has been the person most responsible for the continuing success of the Knoxville Symphony Orchestra. He was the key leader in the process of remodeling both St. John's Cathedral and Cherokee Country Club. He has been very active in many different roles in St. John's Cathedral.

Ben Landers was the CEO for United Way for twenty-six years. During his tenure at United Way, giving grew from $6,000,000 to $13,450,000.

Rodney Lawler is a longtime Knoxville real estate developer. He is the person most responsible for starting Project Grad. In addition, the success of Young Life in Knoxville has been due mainly to the dedicated leadership of Rodney and his wife, Dell.

Rob McCabe was a protégé of Jimmy Smith at the old Park National Bank. Afterward, he went to First American Bank in Nashville and then founded Pinnacle National Bank in 2001, which is currently the largest Tennessee-owned bank. Rob is the leading business leader in the Nashville area. Among many other endeavors, he has served as the President of the Chamber and as the Chairman for the committee that oversaw Nashville's hosting of the NFL Draft in 2019.

Steve Mangum is the Dean of the Haslam College of Business. Steve came to University of Tennessee from Ohio State in 2013. Under his leadership, the College of Business has improved tremendously and is now ranked twenty-seventh among public universities in undergraduate programs and twenty-first in MBA programs.

Sharon Pryse founded the Trust Company of Tennessee, which is now a business that manages over four billion dollars. She has been President of the Chamber and very active in many organizations including United Way, Zoo Knoxville, Friends of the Smokies, and the Knoxville Symphony. She has also been the long-time Treasurer of St. John's Cathedral.

Before graduating from Duke Law School, Chip Robie was an undergraduate at Harvard University where he was an All-American squash player. He has had an outstanding career in wealth management starting with United Asset Management, then moving to Putnam Investments, and is now working at Eagle Capital Management. He has been the Chief Operating Officer of each of these companies.

Tammy White became the CEO of Leadership Knoxville in 2009. She has done a remarkable job. In its thirty-five year history, Leadership Knoxville now has 3,877 graduates.

Again, there is no way I could thank everyone, but I hope that throughout the course of this book and these acknowledgements, you have met some of the co-pilots who have enriched our family, our company, our community, and our lives. A special thanks goes out to all of my friends and family who took the time to graciously add their thoughts to this book in the Afterword. God has blessed me in so many ways in this life, but it is most definitely the people around me who have made me the luckiest man alive.

Enjoy some of their perspectives … I know I have.

IN OTHERS' WORDS

Stories and Perspectives from Friends and Family

JIMMY HASLAM
Son

JIM HASLAM MIGHT BE MY DAD, BUT WE REALLY HAVE MORE OF A *best friend* kind of relationship. Maybe it's because I'm the oldest child or because we have similar personalities and interests—or maybe it's because my dad has always known how to stay young at heart.

I think people sometimes see Dad as this big, intimidating figure: Big Jim. But growing up in our family, it was like having four children, Dad being the fourth child (or perhaps the first child, depending on your point of view). My mom had to keep everything somewhat sane because the rest of us, including Dad, were always in motion with sports, pranks, banter, and just general fun. That was normal life as Jim Haslam's children.

It is not uncommon for kids to want to have friends over to the house or come on vacation with them. It is also not uncommon for parents to sometimes say no to these requests. But for Dad, the more people we had at our house and the more people we took on vacation, the more fun it would be. This philosophy began when I was very young and continued all the way through college. This meant my friends were also his friends—and vice versa.

Having one's friends around one's father had its advantages and disadvantages. I actually don't remember this story, but Dad tells it often and I'm sure it's probably true. When I had been in first grade for only about two weeks, Dad told me to invite a friend from school to go with us to Gatlinburg over a weekend. My best friend was Charles Slatery, who lived one street over from us. We are still great friends today, and he loves this story for reasons you'll soon understand.

We all loaded up in our family station wagon and headed for Gatlinburg. On the way, there were many billboards and barn roofs that had various advertisements painted or printed on them. Well, Charles could read every sign he saw. I, on the other hand, couldn't read at all.

Back then, there were no pre-K or kindergarten programs, which meant you learned to read in first grade—and we had only just started the school year.

Apparently, Dad had a concerned expression on his face, so my mom asked him about it. "Cynthia, I think Jimmy's kind of dumb," he whispered. "Charles can read every sign, and Jimmy can't read anything!"

Two weeks later, there was a play at school and Charles was chosen to read the Bible out loud. It soon became apparent to everyone present that he was the only kid in first grade who could read. This made my dad feel better, and we all laugh about it to this day.

He has a lot of dirt on me, but I have my own embarrassing stories on him as well. Dad grew up in the North primarily and, for whatever reason, he never learned to swim. I had an aunt named Cynthia, the same name as my mom and daughter. I vividly remember Aunt Cynthia teaching me—and Dad—how to swim at the same time . . . one student as an eight-year-old boy and the other as a thirty-something-year-old man. He would probably deny this, but it is true.

The central event of our early years was obviously the sudden death of my mother in 1974. I was a junior in college at UT at the time, Ann was a freshman, and Bill was a junior in high school. I can still recall the experience as if it were yesterday. Something of that magnitude really sticks with you, especially at such a formative age. This probably also explains some of the lifelong friends I made in college, most of whom I'm still close to today—guys like Bob Corker, Bobby Reagan, Jett Andrick, and Bob Talbot. They were there with me—and *for* me—through the whole ordeal.

Right after Mom died, Dad was clearly struggling. At the time, I was living in a little house on his property with a couple of fraternity brothers, while two or three other fraternity brothers were living up at his house. I'm not sure how good it was for the house, but it was really good for Dad because we all hung out with him all the time. We had a tennis court and a basketball court, so we were always playing sports together—with Dad right in the middle of it all. I think it was good for him to be around my friends.

My college buddies were tons of fun and super high energy. Sometimes, on Sunday afternoons when the weather was good and after we'd probably been out later than we should have been the night before, we'd just hang out at the pool, and Dad would join us. I remember multiple times when he gathered everyone around and said something like, "I've observed all you guys, and I have confidence that each of you is going to do reasonably well in life. I just want to make sure you remember to give back to the communities you're involved in."

Bill eventually became the Governor, Bob Corker became a United States Senator, and the rest have done reasonably well in life. They probably would have done well anyway, but if you ask Bob Corker or Bobby Reagan—and probably most of the guys—they can remember Dad giving us these talks. I think he was good for them because he was really on the rise as a prominent businessman, which meant that everyone knew how he gave back to the community. However, I think these guys were good for him as well.

My dad doesn't drink, doesn't smoke, and doesn't have a lot of hobbies. His hobbies are work, faith, family, and friends; he doesn't even play golf. He played a little tennis and liked to exercise, but he didn't have a lot to do after Mom died. It was hard to watch him because he wasn't a guy who went out a lot socially—his family had been his social life.

Natalie was going through a divorce at the time and her first husband eventually passed away several years later. When she and Dad ended up getting married, it was so much fun because we all knew Natalie so well, and we loved her. This is also when we gained three stepsisters. Jennie is about the same age as Ann, while Susan and Carol are a bit younger— closer to Bill's age. We all already knew one another very well, so it was a great fit and very healing for Dad, as well as the rest of us. Mom's passing was a terrible tragedy and remains a painful subject to this day, but we have been grateful that so many people have come together as a family, which is a God thing.

From a work perspective, my dad has taught me so much. He continues to be an incredible partner to work with. One of the things that has kept us very close to each other is that even today at eighty-nine years old, Dad still comes into work every day. He remains the keeper of the culture at Pilot. Between my work with the Browns, traveling to our various stores, and constantly being on the lookout for future Pilot real estate, I come to the Pilot Company offices about a day and a half each week. Even though it may not be every day, the fact that we both still work here gives us a chance to talk constantly.

Sometimes we visit for ten minutes. Other times, it might be for an hour and a half. Regardless, our work relationship gives us a chance to stay in contact, which is something we both love. I think we would have been really close anyway because we're so much alike and such good friends, but we're even closer because we work together, which is not something everyone can say about their dad . . . especially when he is at the age of eighty-nine.

When we started working together, Pilot only had around seventy-five gas stations. Much of our time was spent traveling around the southeastern United States looking for more locations. Many of our memories are tethered to these trips. For example, we had two gas stations located between Blacksburg and Pearisburg, Virginia. It was on that forty-minute drive between these two locations when I told Dad that Dee and I were getting married. I'd bet you a dollar that if you ask him when I told him I was getting married, he'd say between Pearisburg and Blacksburg.

Dad has done an unbelievable job of involving his family in the company. Many times when a father is the founder, he doesn't want to give his children any real responsibility, but this has never been the case with my dad. I gleaned a lot from my experiences in school and I had already been working for Pilot during much of this time. Even so, I was still only twenty-two years old. I didn't know anything about anything. At the time, the gasoline business was changing to the point that you couldn't *just* be in the gasoline business anymore. People expected more.

Within a few months of my coming to Pilot, Dad told me that we needed to get into the convenience store business. This was something we had already agreed upon. However, I was stunned when Dad said that *I* should figure out how to do it. I told him I didn't even know where to begin, so he connected me with five respected businessmen from across the country—each knowing something about the travel center business—that I could talk to. I learned so much from these conversations and experiences because Dad let me try things, even if it meant I might fail at first. He helped me succeed by actually helping me learn how to do the job, not just throwing me to the wolves.

Bill and I both served on Pilot's board at very young ages, but even when we were very young, Dad always took us everywhere with him, introducing us to as many experiences as he could, including politics. Growing up, we had the pleasure of meeting government leaders such as Howard Baker, Lamar Alexander, and many others. This exposure to the political side of the world deeply impacted both Bill and myself.

Bill, of course, ended up running for office; I never did. Regardless, Dad exposed us all to so many things that left a lasting mark on our lives. Business, politics, and sports were the practical skills and experiences he gave us—the backdrop of our daily lives. Or course, faith and family were the main pillars upon which all these other things were built. Dad modeled for us all what it means to be a good husband, father, and friend.

I can remember being in Tempe, Arizona, when Tennessee won the National Championship in 1998. After the game, we came back to the hotel around midnight to find Dad and Natalie hanging out with Hank Lauricella and his wife, Betty. We opened the door to their suite and were greeted by the loudest laughing you've ever heard in your life. Here they were—my Dad, with all of his many accomplishments, hanging with his old buddy, who was a Hall of Famer. They had won a championship together in 1951, and you could just tell that the connection had only strengthened over the years that followed. Natalie and Betty were also impressive: one was Miss Tennessee in 1951, and the other was Miss Tennessee in 1952.

There was no alcohol present, but their spirits were high. It was a memorable moment for me as they gathered around a big table with a gorgeous setting in the middle. It warmed my heart watching and hearing them carry on together because they all loved Tennessee—and one another—so very much.

That is my Dad: a man of big laughter, high integrity, gifted leadership, extreme generosity, and above all, a heart of gold. I love him dearly.

ANN BAILEY
Daughter

JIM HASLAM HAS ALWAYS BEEN THE BEST DAD A GIRL COULD HAVE. The simple way he cares for us has taught me so much about life. He's a very faith-centered man and has worked hard his entire life. He is also a deeply committed family person who sets high standards for himself and others. I think all his kids would agree that growing up, he was the kind of father anyone would wish for.

But I am so blessed to have him as *my* dad.

Dad is incredibly fun, and truth be told, he has always been this way. When I was young, he had to travel quite a bit, usually leaving on Sunday nights or Monday mornings. Despite all these challenges to his schedule, I never remember him missing a single event of mine. He might not have liked them all (he thought swim meets were the most boring events on the planet), but he still made it to every one. I attended a private school that hosted "Dads' Nights" where each father would write a poem or a few thoughts about his child. While some dads participated reluctantly, my dad was all-in on these kinds of things. He was all-in on our lives in general—a wholehearted man in every way.

Dad truthfully is one of the funniest people in the world. More than any human being I've ever known, he constantly laughs at himself. He even gets tickled at himself in his worst moments—at times when most people would clam up or shut down. But he also knows how to be serious when it matters, always ending every conversation with, "If you need me, I'm here." This is a real promise, and he always follows through on it. Right before he was slated to have triple bypass surgery, he called and said, "Now, if y'all need me, call me." And he meant it.

He is one of the most successful businessmen of our era, but he doesn't think of himself as such. He sees himself as a simple football player who came to Tennessee and got lucky. He knows he has been blessed by his situation and is eternally grateful.

My husband, Steve, and I are often with him when he gets together with his old buddies from the 1950s. They laugh and carry on as if everything they are reminiscing about happened yesterday— his gratitude for these earlier times never ceases. In fact, Dad appreciates and enjoys his life more than any person I know. To this day, my friends often ask me to invite my dad over to one of our gatherings or events because they know he'll bring so much fun and energy to any occasion.

My brothers, Jimmy and Bill, have had a business relationship with Dad, but I've had a different relationship with him, especially since our mother died. I took care of him for about a year, so we have a different and unique bond than what he shares with my brothers. That's probably true for most fathers and daughters.

I have had serious health problems that have required surgical intervention. Years ago, we found out I was suffering from a dissected aorta. This was the same condition that no doubt caused my mother's death, so you can imagine how hard this was on my dad. Through it all, he was extremely encouraging. When I was at the Cleveland Clinic, he would often fly up for the day just to see me. He is so compassionate with a deep love for his kids and his wife.

Dad and I talk every single day. Recently, Steve and I went out of the country on a cruise and Dad bought me a satellite phone, just in case the phone service on the boat stopped working. Talking to my dad is that important to both of us.

If you walk into his office, you will immediately see a life-sized cardboard cutout of me by his desk. It is a sight to behold, but there's a funny reason why it's there. Right after Bill was elected Governor, we were celebrating Easter down at the beach. I was joking with Jimmy that there are fifty-five pictures of Bill in Dad's office and only two pictures of me. We all playfully gave Dad grief about it.

A few weeks later, I was about to pull off a surprise sixtieth birthday party for a friend when Dad called. His voice was very determined, which alarmed me. If Dad ever says, "I really need you to come down here," you drop whatever you're doing and go right then.

"Dad?" I said, "Are you sick?

"No."

"Well, have I done something?"

"No, but it's very important that you come over here." He was using his stern voice, so I went immediately. When I got there, I discovered the huge picture of me that now dwarfs everyone else's in the office. Everyone who walks into his office gets tickled—and sometimes they think I'm actually standing there. It's a great running joke.

My husband would tell you Jim Haslam is the best father-in-law in the world. They are very close; he is as crazy about Dad as I am. We all love that he brings such fun and energy to our lives, even though life hasn't always been fun.

About five or six days after our mother died, Dad sat the three of us children down at breakfast and encouraged us that we would eventually have to go back out and face the world again. He knew we were hurting, but he gave us hope that we would be able to function again someday. He said the world was not going to feel sorry for us for long because this was just a part of life. I think his generation, which lived through various wars and atrocities, has a different perspective on death and suffering.

Looking back, I can't help but admire the way he handled himself after our mother died. He gave strength to us throughout the whole experience. Our family was all that we really had left to depend on, and now I know that, for the rest of my life, both my brothers will always be there for me. I think Dad really instilled such a strong sense of family in us during this time, no doubt feeling such a deep responsibility for the three of us.

Dad can be serious, but usually not for long. After Mother died and before he married Natalie, quite a few Sigma Chi brothers were living with Jimmy at our house. One day when Dad came home from work, they were outside goofing around with water hoses. When he got out of the car, they all came at him and hosed him down. He was still wearing his suit! Of course, he loved every minute of it.

Dad has also taught us to help others. Steve and I have been honored to have opportunities to serve at our church, specifically to head up our stewardship ministry. Over the past seven or eight years, Dad has been our coach throughout all these endeavors. He is my mentor and a wonderful example to our church, which is one of the reasons he is so highly respected.

He may be respected, but he is still just a redneck at heart. Years and years ago, Dad took Jimmy and Bill along for a business trip. They also had tickets to go to a baseball game. The game must have been hot because Dad and the boys took off their shirts. I'm serious: Dad was literally shirtless with dress pants on.

When he came home, Mom asked him if it was hot at the game and if he had taken his shirt off. He denied it until she told him she had seen them on the television broadcast of the game. We have laughed for years about Dad's shirtless secret.

And he is obviously "Mr. University of Tennessee." One year, Steve and Natalie conspired to get the Pride of the Southland Marching Band over to the house to surprise him for his birthday. Of course, Dad absolutely loved it. Dad truly believes that the university shaped him by teaching him so much about the right way to live his life. Life with General Neyland, his fellow players, and their shared experiences on the football field set for him a high standard—one that he never stopped pursuing after college. Among other convictions, Dad has never had a drink, which I think is the result of the powerful impact these years of discipline and standard-setting had on his life. He sets the highest standards for himself of any person I know.

He is also a wonderful note writer, which also includes sending texts or leaving messages. When you call him, he always answers his phone, letting you know he's never too busy for you. This is an unbelievable trait in today's world because I know there are a lot of demands on this time.

He is also athletic and active. He was always an avid runner and, in his later years, a cyclist. Dad would often wear running clothes under his suits so that, after church or work, he could simply take off his top layer and start running wherever he wanted to go.

After Mother died, Dad and I would drive to church together and he would always wear his running clothes under his suit. I would drive home after church, stopping to pick up lunch on the way. He would then run home and we would eat lunch together. One day, he asked me to pick up McDonald's and told me to get some money out of his wallet to pay for it. When I opened it, all he had were hundreds, so I took a hundred, bought lunch (it was interesting breaking a hundred dollar bill in a McDonald's in the mid-1970s), and put the change back into his wallet.

After he made it home, he came downstairs and claimed that I had not put the money back. He was very upset, but we both knew it wasn't really about the money. It had been such a hard experience for us—the lowest point in our lives. I told him that I had absolutely put it back. He was still upset, but instead of fighting with me, he went outside and got on the riding lawn mower, mowing every inch of our yard.

Later that afternoon, he came back into my room and said, "It takes a big man to admit when he's wrong. I found my money and I'm sorry."

I wasn't surprised. That is my dad. He truly is a big man in every sense of the word. He has been an anchor to our family, an example to our children, and my hero for life.

BILL HASLAM
Son

Since I had the honor of writing the foreword for this book, I will pick up where I left off and add a few more stories and reflections. I can truthfully say that, of all the people I've worked with in business, government, or community agencies over the years, I've never met anyone who gives from such a selfless place as Jim Haslam. Dad is, like the rest of us, far from perfect, but he is someone who is always thinking about how he can serve the people around him. He has always been a team-first person, even when he was the leader of the team.

When I ran for Mayor the first time, some people thought having his son as the Mayor was just another way for Big Jim to control one more thing in Knoxville. Dad had always been kind of a big deal in Knoxville because of the civic causes he had led. I was probably overly conscious of it. One day, I was out knocking on doors and campaigning when I introduced myself to the homeowner. "Hello, I'm Bill Haslam, and I'm running for Mayor."

"Haslam?" the man asked. "Are you any kin to that Jim Haslam, the one who played football at Tennessee?"

"Yes," I said, bowing up a little as I prepared for the inevitable jab.

"Hmm, whatever happened to him?" he asked.

This still makes me laugh. I guess I was a little hypersensitive because I have always been proud that Jim Haslam is my dad. To this day, it is just so much fun to be with him, as everyone who knows him will attest.

For family vacations, we would often drive to Myrtle Beach, South Carolina, or Daytona Beach, Florida. Of course, we would drive the long way in our station wagon because Dad always needed to visit some of our gas stations along the way or take a look at one of our competitor's stores. Thus a trip that would normally take eight or nine hours would take us twelve or thirteen.

To make the most of the time, we would sing college fight songs most of the way. Even today, Tennessee will be playing another team in football and I will just randomly sing the opposing team's fight song, which always surprises whoever is sitting with me.

As children, when we were playing with any of the kids in our neighborhood, whether it was touch football, softball, basketball, or kickball, Dad was always the pitcher, referee, or whatever other role was needed. He was always there in our front yard, which became the favorite neighborhood gathering spot—not because of Jimmy, Ann, or myself, but because of Dad. Kids would say, "Let's go to your house. Your dad will be there!"

You can tell a lot about a person by the fact that people feel comfortable enough to give him or her silly nicknames. Once in the 1960s when Jimmy was about eleven years old, he got a haircut and Dad sent him back in because he didn't think it was short enough.

"Dad," Jimmy protested, "only rednecks make their kids cut their hair this short!"

Dad replied, "Well, then, I guess I'm a neck, and that's just what you'll have to be too!"

After that, we called Dad *Neck* for about ten years.

We used to all work out together, and when we'd do chin-ups, we would call out the name of an old Yankees player whose number corresponded with the number of reps we were about to attempt. We did this because Dad grew up a New York Yankees fan. So if you wanted to do seven chin-ups, you'd say "Mickey Mantle!" Five was Joe DiMaggio—and so forth and so on. One time, Dad yelled out "Clete Boyer!" No one but him even knew who that was, so we started calling him *Cletey* after that.

I've also had the honor of calling him *Boss*. It is common for company founders to dig their fingers into the business and hold on to the bitter end, but our dad was incredibly generous about letting us have significant leadership roles in the company early in our careers. In hindsight, he might have even given us a little too much leeway to lead in our twenties and thirties, but he never let us fall so far that he wasn't there to catch us. It was a great training experience because, through thick and thin, he always had our backs.

As a business person, it was interesting to grow up as Jim Haslam's son and then begin my own career under his leadership. He taught me three things about business. The first is that you better know the numbers of your business, whatever it might be. When I was involved in government, I would often meet business people who would say, "I'm just not a numbers person, so I'll let someone else figure that part out."

This has always struck me as the wrong way to do business. I believe that you must understand the fundamentals of your operation—that is, how the financials work. You don't have to be a financial analyst with an MBA, but if you don't understand the basics of how the numbers work, you're never going to be effective in any enterprise, whether it's a school, business, elected office, or even a church.

Secondly, it only took a small amount of time working with Dad to know that, if you get relationships right, most other things tend to work out well. This means treating people the right way all the time. This was a simple lesson to learn—all you had to do was watch the way Dad treated people. Always kind. Always respectful.

The third business lesson I learned from my dad was about being diligent to find ways to solve problems. If you were to ask me about his greatest strength, I would say it is this: if there is a problem in his vicinity, he takes responsibility for solving it. If there's a weakness in this, it's that he sometimes thinks that, given the chance, he can solve any problem out there. I have often laughed because it seems he thinks if he could only get the right people in the room, he could solve any problem from peace in the Middle East to national healthcare.

Part of this drive to solve problems comes from the fact that he is an optimist with every fiber of his being. When he was coaching my Little League teams, there were some kids whom you knew were headed in a dangerous direction with their life choices. Even so, Dad remained encouraging and would never let them be labeled as "bad" kids. He would say that they just needed to be around different people and have a little more encouragement from a caring adult. This has always been the way he sees the world.

Another obvious lesson I've learned from him is that life is better when you're not living it only for yourself. Many people find it difficult to learn how to tithe or how to get involved in nonprofit or charitable endeavors. When I first began to think seriously about my own spiritual journey, giving and generosity—things that are sometimes challenging for young or new believers—felt more natural for me to embrace. I had simply grown up watching my dad live his life as a generous giver…and certain things are better *caught* than *taught*.

Without a doubt, the lowest point of Dad's business career was when Pilot came under investigation. It was not just a kick in the stomach; it was a *repeated* kick in the stomach. I think the whole thing was so painful to him because he is such a *do the right thing* person. And, when you start a company, you can't help but feel a different level of identity, ownership, and attachment to it. At the time, Dad had invested fifty-five years of his life into Pilot, so he cared deeply what kind of company it was—and what kind of company it would remain.

He was on vacation at the beach when it all went down. While he rushed home the next day, I think he quickly realized it was not his role to dive in and sort everything out. He knew he had to set his problem-solving skills to the side and focus on ensuring that those who worked there could still feel confident about their company.

Dad dedicated himself to going around to all of the offices and travel centers to tell the team members in person that everything was going to be okay. Whereas most leaders in painful moments tend to retreat or bury themselves under work (or under the covers), Dad came out into the open so he could play the role he was born to play: Encourager-In-Chief. His attitude spoke to a lot of people when they needed it most.

This was not a problem he could solve, but he realized his demeanor was something he *could* control. He often says that Pilot came out of that ordeal a much better company—he means this with all his heart, mainly because it is true. In my opinion, one of the reasons it is true is because Dad maintained strong and steady leadership from start to finish.

Looking ahead for Pilot, Berkshire Hathaway will become the majority owner in 2023. Even this transaction tells you a lot about Jim Haslam. Truthfully, if you wanted to simply maximize the money you could make, you wouldn't sell to Berkshire. They are not going to pay top dollar; they've earned a reputation as great investors for a reason. But what we did get with Berkshire is an investor who wants Pilot to keep running its business as it has for over fifty years, which includes ensuring that it remains in Knoxville with the same commitment to its people and communities. This speaks to who he is and the concern he has for the team members of Pilot and the communities in which they live.

Another extraordinary aspect of my dad is that his children, grand-children, step-grandchildren, great-grandchildren—and everyone in between—all have their own special relationships with him in varying ways, especially depending on how much they get to see him. The generation below ours feels such an authentic attachment to him, which is something you don't see very often these days. He is a man in his late eighties deeply connecting with people in their twenties and thirties.

I will receive a letter from Dad three, four, and sometimes five times a year, just telling me how much he loves me and how proud he is of me. Every year at Christmas, he writes a letter to every one of his children and grandchildren. In these letters, he recaps the year in a bigger picture for the family, but also for that individual, laying out what happened in his or her life. It always ends with how much he loves that person and how proud he is of them. I have a stack of those letters. My kids have a stack of those letters. My wife, Crissy, has a stack of those letters, as do all the other members of our family.

I was talking with a group of guys one day and somehow one of these letters came up in conversation. One of them responded with, "Wow! Your dad tells you how much he loves you and how proud he is of you every year?"

"No," I said, "he tells me all the time, but he puts it in writing at least four times a year." Until you get older and talk to other men, you just don't realize how rare it is for men to hear these kinds of things from their fathers consistently. When it comes to having a father who is supportive, affirming, and loving, I hit the lottery.

I could go on telling stories about my dad and his life and impact for a long time. His influence cannot be easily summed up or measured. His true impact is written in my life, the lives of other members of our family, and in countless lives that are better because of Jim Haslam.

NATALIE HASLAM
Wife

It's hard to describe Jim Haslam without using the word *caretaker*. He has always been a caretaker, caring well for his family, his mother up to the point of her death, and his sisters. As his wife, I can truthfully say he is the most loving and caring man I've ever met. He wakes up with a smile every morning, even though it takes me about three cups of coffee to get there. A dedicated father and husband, he is so much fun to be with. I am blessed to be his wife.

Jim has accomplished many incredible things in his life, so much so that we have heard over the years that some people get nervous about meeting him. This means they have no idea how easy he is and how much he loves people. In fact, I think people are surprised when they get to know him because they discover that he's such a good guy. He's just one of us, which is wonderful.

Cynthia, Jim's late wife and the mother of his children, was one of my dearest friends from childhood. When we were all at UT, there were only five thousand students, so everybody knew everybody else. Jim was just a friend back then and, if you ever would have told me that we would be married someday, I wouldn't have believed it.

I have lived in Knoxville my entire life. I attended Sequoyah School in the Sequoyah Hills neighborhood. Cynthia came to my school in the third grade and we became lifelong friends. General Neyland's sons, Lewis and Bob Neyland, also attended school with us.

When we went to college, Cynthia became a Tri Delt and I became a Chi Omega. All the girls my age who were from Knoxville usually did not live in the dormitories. The war had barely been over for a few years when we started college, and our parents weren't going to pay for room and board when there was room and board at home.

Because we didn't live on campus, we didn't hang out on Cumberland Avenue (the strip) very much. We did hang around the fraternity houses, however. It was a different time then, and girls had to be home early. In fact, if you were a female freshman living on campus at UT, you had to be in your dormitory by 9:15 p.m. except on weekends. I didn't live on campus, but my parents were just as strict about my curfew.

While we didn't hang out around campus as much as some of the others, the football players certainly did. Some of them had cars, even though they weren't supposed to. They just had to keep them hidden from General Neyland, which didn't always work out. Jim and one of his best friends, Hank Lauricella, a Heisman runner-up, once had a close call over the car issue. Hank's future wife, Betty, became one of my best friends when we were freshmen. Hank has since passed away, but Betty still lives in New Orleans and remains a wonderful friend of ours.

I majored in French, though I am far from fluent. This is something Jim used to give me a hard time about; that is, until we took a trip to France. Jim was driving in Paris, and we were going around the Arc de Triomphe. Needless to say, it was scary. We were with some friends, and I was riding in the back seat. We had heard about a restaurant away from the city, and we wanted to go there for lunch. But when we got to the little town where it supposedly was, we couldn't find it.

Jim practically pulled up on the sidewalk and used his big voice to ask a man standing there—in English, of course. The man was puzzled by his questions, so Jim turned to me and said, "Natalie, say something to him." I asked him in French where the restaurant was and he told me. That was a long time ago, but Jim has never again teased me about my inability to speak French.

Regardless of our majors, our time at UT was very special. I graduated in three years, but in those three years, we went to three huge bowl games that Jim played in. We were also number-one in the nation, so it was a time like no other, especially when you consider how young we were. To that end, Jim's college nickname was *Youngin'*. He was only seventeen when he came to school. Of course, many veterans were coming home from the war and enrolling in school, and I think being around some of these older men was a real education for Youngin'.

Cynthia and I remained close friends after she married Jim. It was a devastating day when Ann called me with the news that she had passed away. I got there as quickly as I could. Thankfully, she had died peacefully. It was tough on everyone, but, in the months that followed, the whole family responded with courage and grace.

I was so surprised when Jim and I started dating. I think Ann might have been in a hurry for it to happen because Jim had put quite a bit on her. She had to be the family hostess, and I'm sure she was ready for someone else to take over that role. But the time flew by and dating Jim was a lot of fun.

We made our first appearance as a couple at a UT game we attended with some good friends of ours. Back then, the games always started at 2:00 p.m. and were always over by 4:00 p.m. It was wonderful. We had plans to go to Jim's house for dinner afterward, and I needed a head of lettuce from the store to make a salad.

I think Jim felt funny the whole day because we were out together and everyone was looking at us. The town was a lot smaller, and the pressure was kind of traumatic for Jim. Lo and behold, he came out of the store with a big head of cabbage instead of lettuce. He laughs about that all the time, but eventually, we settled into this relationship and have had many, many wonderful years together.

After we were married, he embraced my girls, of course. He had known them since birth. Actually, one of my girls is his goddaughter and Ann is my goddaughter. Jim has always been so very inclusive, and he means a great deal to all three of my children. He changed their lives, as well as mine.

We've now been married more than forty-four years, and I can tell you that, as wonderful as he is, no one is perfect. If I had to name one thing that may not be perfect about him, it would be that he is really good at seeing the big picture, but he can sometimes miss the details. This can be a good thing or a bad thing depending on the situation.

He will come in and say, "Oh, when did you get that picture?"

"Well," I'll reply, "it's been hanging on the wall for three months now."

But even this "flaw" can work to my advantage because he doesn't notice if my hair is a little out of place. In all seriousness, we're so entirely different, but our differences complement each other. It is amazing that we get along like we do because he's interested in sports and business—and, while I do love to watch and attend basketball games, I am not into sports like he is. I'd rather be reading, hiking in the mountains, or gardening—not that I can do all these things anymore.

Even so, we completely agree on the big things in life like church, trying to set a good example for our kids, and giving back to the community. I think our relationship amazes us both because we are so very different, yet so very happy together. I am just so proud of him for the things he has accomplished (sometimes by himself) and for the kind of person he is.

Above all, I'm extremely proud to bear his name.

JENNIE MCCABE, SUSAN ROBIE AND CAROL PATTISON
Stepdaughters

YOU MAY KNOW HIM AS MR. HASLAM OR BIG JIM, BUT WE HAVE always known him as Hazzie. We don't have a single "first" memory of Hazzie because even before he was our stepfather, he was a large presence in our lives as we often went on family trips together. We would gather at their house on Scenic Drive every Fourth of July.

At those gatherings, Hazzie would give "the little girls" (Susan and Carol) "jumps." We would run to him shouting "Jumps, Hazzie!" and he would toss each of us high into the air over his head. It was a sad, sad day when Susan got too heavy for jumps, but Carol, the youngest, still made the cut. As the oldest sister, Jennie was unfortunately always too old for jumps.

Hazzie has never had a drink of alcohol or smoked a cigarette in his entire life, although he has always been generous in ordering us fine wines at restaurant dinners.

We're still amazed that he knows all the words to every college fight song ever written, which is not a small feat. He even knows all the camp songs to the summer camps that each of his children attended. And though he can't sing in tune or clap to a beat, he does it all anyway with great gusto.

There is a tender, childlike quality to him that the world rarely sees. In high school when either Carol or Susan would get upset about something, he would come into our rooms at night and sing a little song called "Open, Shut Them"—complete with hand gestures. It was clearly a song for toddlers, but by the end of it, we would be laughing so hysterically that we had forgotten our woes.

While Susan and Carol were living in "the kennels"—the back part of the house—we often had sleepovers with friends. Our friends grew to be playfully wary of Saturday-morning breakfasts with Hazzie because he would go around the table and ask each girl to report on how many kisses they had received the night before. This was known as a "category check," and it was hilarious, though sometimes embarrassing. We also remember that Hazzie had the first car phone in Knoxville. His huge Cadillac had a strange-looking antenna coming out the back. We got such a kick out of him sitting in the car in the driveway and calling the house from that shoebox of a phone.

We are so grateful for the most special relationship that Hazzie has with our mother. When you are around them, you can sense the mutual respect and love they have for each other. People can't help but notice it. He has introduced her to the worlds of politics, business, and sports, while she has exposed him to the arts and culture. He often marvels that now he even enjoys going to the symphony, though he still likes to leave at "halftime."

We have all benefited from his love and the example he has set. He truly lives by the maxim that it is more blessed to give than to receive. Hazzie has been an incredible role model and each day, and he chooses to be happy. He has taught us how to treat others and the importance of giving back to the community.

PEYTON MANNING

University of Tennessee Quarterback (1994–1997)

Jim Haslam is one of the finest men I've ever known. My connection to Mr. Haslam came through another player from Louisiana, the All-American Hank Lauricella. My dad knew Hank, so we formed a bond when I went to Tennessee because we were both UT quarterbacks from New Orleans.

Of course, Jim and Hank were best friends—you could tell that they genuinely loved each other. I can remember my dad talking about being with them and how they would laugh nonstop. They truly enjoyed each other's company. Their wives were also the best of friends. Hank was certainly the link between our family and the Haslams.

My time with Mr. Haslam over the years has proven to me beyond a shadow of a doubt that not only is he one of the greatest businessmen this country has ever seen, but, also the biggest Tennessee fan and supporter who has ever lived. I think I could make a pretty convincing argument for this.

To be clear, I don't just mean that he is a supporter of only the athletic department or football. Mr. Haslam loves *the entire university* in a way that is both authentic and contagious. Every time I'm around him, we always talk about the current football team, as well as the old players— and the depth of these conversations energizes me. When it comes to Tennessee athletics—and really *any* topic—his mind is as sharp as a tack and he has unbelievable recall. I truly enjoy these times.

Mr. Haslam also values integrity in ways that most people will never know—because he is too humble to tout it. During my sophomore year, we were playing Kentucky in Lexington, and my dad received a phone call from Mr. Haslam. Mr. Haslam told my dad that he was flying down to New Orleans on his plane to pick up Hank Lauricella and his wife, Betty, and he wanted to know if my mom and dad wanted to catch a ride with them to Lexington to watch me play. It was a very nice gesture and my dad said yes.

But in typical Jim Haslam fashion, he called my dad back the next day and told him that while he was not retracting his offer, he had thought about it more and called Coach Dickey, the Athletic Director, to seek counsel on the matter. He didn't want to inadvertently violate any NCAA rules by transporting my parents, which could cause a lot of trouble for the university and my family. Coach Dickey had suggested that my parents simply pay their portion of the fuel and other expenses for the flight.

Jim passed this wisdom along to my dad to keep everything on the up-and-up. My dad took him up on this second offer and they still flew together to the game. The bottom line is that no one would have known anything about this plane ride, but Jim Haslam has always been that concerned about doing everything he does with integrity, to the best of his ability.

I have enjoyed a friendship with him and also with his family. Just recently, I sent a video to Mr. Haslam, Jimmy, and Bill—something light and fun just to wish them well during the holidays. We all do various things in the Knoxville community, so we have fairly consistent communication throughout the year both in-person and through our ongoing group text.

When it comes to fundraising for worthy causes, Mr. Haslam is second-to-none. He won't take "no" for an answer, mainly because he is already supporting whatever cause, candidate, or campaign for which he is raising money. In 2005, when I was still in Indianapolis, Mr. Haslam, along with the University President and the Athletic Director at the time, flew to Denver during a University of Tennessee capital campaign to meet with a specific donor about developing future athletic facilities. They asked me to tag along and picked me up at the airport in Indianapolis on their way.

That evening, we went to a Rockies game to see Todd Helton play. Todd's mother used to work for Pilot, and Mr. Haslam was always very kind and loving to her, so there was a great connection there. Afterward, we had dinner with the prospective donor. It was yet another time I was able to witness the honed fundraising skills of Jim Haslam. He is a smooth operator, but it is only because his passion for Tennessee comes out so clearly. I remember he was asking the donor for a significant number—so significant that I wanted to be in the room when he asked for it. All told, I don't know whether he was able to secure the requested donation or not, but I can promise you that he was able to secure something substantial, so it was a successful meeting.

Recently I attended what could be best described as a kind of *State of the Union* meeting for the Tennessee Athletic Department at Blackberry Farm. It was a meeting to communicate progress and goals with supporters and donors. There was a man there in the beer business whose father had been good friends with Mr. Haslam in his past. Mr. Haslam told both of us a story of a letter he once wrote to his friend—this guy's dad—regarding a fundraising endeavor for the Knoxville Boys and Girls Club. Of course, Jim and Natalie Haslam were leading the campaign because no one has been more philanthropic and generous to so many causes than them. For the sake of the story, I'll just call the gentleman "George." In his letter, Mr. Haslam said, "George, as you know, the good Lord has blessed both you and me in so many ways. So Natalie and I will be giving 'X' to the Boys and Girls Club."

Mr. Haslam said George wrote back to him: "Jim, the Lord has blessed you more than he has me, so I will be giving 'X' amount instead of how much you are giving." If you've never heard Jim Haslam laugh, then it's hard to describe. Needless to say, he laughed hard when he told us this story. He thought his friend's answer was quick and clever, attributes he appreciates. Regardless, he was successful in raising funds for yet another cause dear to his heart.

Mr. Haslam has always been supportive and encouraging, watching me play both in college and in the NFL. He would fly up to Indianapolis several times a year for games and would always check in with me, just to see how I was doing. He also always sent me messages either of congratulations or consolation after games.

Even before I retired, I would always try to go back to Tennessee for certain football games on bye weekends. Of course, I can do this more nowadays. Regardless, I always try to pop into their box to sit and watch a quarter of the game with the Haslams. However, if you're going to do this, you should know that watching a game with Mr. Haslam is not social time. He is seriously into what's happening on the field, so it's not a time to catch up on niceties. It's a serious box in there—and I have always enjoyed being with them any chance I get.

Finally, if you spend any time at all with Jim Haslam, then you know that he still loves General Neyland. I know that the General had a great impact on so many of his players, but I'm not sure he had a greater impact on anyone more than Jim Haslam. Mr. Haslam still applies so many of the General's principles to his life and business. When you're with him, he is always talking about the General—and I *love* hearing those stories.

Theirs was obviously more than just a coach-player relationship that came to an end as soon as Mr. Haslam stopped playing football. No, Mr. Haslam took to heart everything he learned from the General, so much so that these principles and disciplines are still with him today. I think the fact that the General had such an impact on Jim says a lot about them both.

I can't say enough about Jim Haslam. He has been an incredible friend and a mentor to me, and I'm so very thankful that he is a part of my life.

PHILLIP FULMER

University of Tennessee Football Head Coach (1992–2008)
University of Tennessee Director of Athletics (2017–Present)

LET'S BE CLEAR: WHEN IT COMES TO PHILANTHROPY, AS WELL AS LOVE for and dedication to the University of Tennessee, Jim Haslam is our greatest letterman.

From the time he showed up on campus as a scholarship football player in the late 1940s, he has been a fighter and a leader. I have always heard that he showed up on campus carrying all his belongings in a paper bag. Folklore or not, it adds to his incredible story and how it impacted so many others, including me.

Jim went on to become a team Captain on a national championship team during a great era of Tennessee football. He took those leadership skills from his academic and football experiences and used them to build a successful company, raise a very successful family, greatly impact a city and state, and become a leader and major supporter of his beloved University of Tennessee.

I first met Jim when I came back to Tennessee as an Assistant Coach in the early 1980s. His story, along with his success as an athlete and a businessman, were very impressive. I admired all that Mr. Haslam was achieving while still paying close attention to his university. His extraordinary story—and other stories like his—are what make our university special.

Mr. Haslam came to UT as a first-generation student, played a very team-oriented position as an offensive lineman on some great teams, became a Captain—and did it all while playing for *the* General Neyland. All of this collectively reveals his character, work ethic, toughness, and leadership ability. All of the history of those teams during that era—including the players and coaches—became larger than life to all of us who followed them. They became the standards, positively laying new foundations in Tennessee football history and tradition.

Over the years, Jim and I have shared many fun times together talking about how important our Tennessee football playing experiences have been to us and how this time shaped each of our lives. In those talks, he always reminisces about General Neyland and his assistant coaches—and I am always fascinated, eager to soak up the stories. He shares about how important it was that he stayed in college. This helped him move toward all that he wanted from life, and being at UT was much better than going home. He took advantage of his opportunities and made his life, his family, and all of the world around UT a better place to be.

Jim approaches life with an extremely positive outlook. He is a caring and generous man who has truly made Knoxville and the state of Tennessee a better place to live. He has changed lives in ways that the public will never know about. He cares for children, the elderly, and is the most philanthropic person I know. Jim's energy and heart to serve spill over into his family as well. It is amazing to see all that his children (and now grandchildren) have accomplished and continue to accomplish—how they are touching so many lives.

I became the Head Football Coach in 1992 and began to have regular interactions with Mr. Haslam and the other trustees. I always came away from those meetings appreciative of his support. He never let a meeting end without asking the question, "What can I do for you?" No matter what it was, philosophical, facility related, or personal, Jim was always willing to try to help in whatever way he could.

I have always really enjoyed it when he quotes General Neyland—and especially his Game Maxims. He believes in them as I do. He learned and practiced the maxims throughout his life. He learned that the team (or company) that makes the fewest mistakes wins. He learned how to fight back when the breaks have gone against him. He learned how to prepare for the moment, how to do the fundaments well, and how to play for the breaks and take advantage when the moment comes. He learned very well, if the breaks go against you, never let up ... put on more steam. He has practiced these all of his adult life.

Bricks and mortar are certainly important parts of what make a university great, but the people who lead, the people who love, and the people who give back are the true foundations. I am extremely appreciative to Jim and his family for all they have done for our university, community, state, and country.

RICK BARNES

University of Tennessee Men's Basketball
Head Coach (2015–Present)

I KNOW IT MAY SOUND STRANGE, BUT I DREAMED ABOUT THIS moment—the moment you would be reading a book about the life and story of Mr. Jim Haslam. I'm not joking; the images appeared in my mind as clear as daylight.

In my dream, I was speaking with him and I said, "Mr. Haslam, I want to read the book about you."

"There's not one," he replied.

I remember feeling shocked and almost offended. "There's not one? Mr. Haslam, you have a story that just has to be told!" Then I woke up.

It was a strange dream indeed, so I called him and told him about it. In his humble way, he sheepishly replied, "Well, don't tell anybody, but we're talking about maybe writing a book." And here we are.

Let me start from the beginning. I spent many years coaching basketball at the University of Texas. Frankly, I always thought I was in control of my life. Consequently, this also meant that I thought I was going to be in Texas forever.

Then one day, all that changed and I found myself being shown the door. At first, I didn't know what was coming next for me and my family, but by the time I was wrapping up my final press conference at the University of Texas, it was clear that I was coming to the University of Tennessee.

Looking back, I can easily see that God brought me here. I found out that I wasn't in control (and never had been), but I also found out that God had a bigger plan for me than I could ever draw up for myself on a whiteboard. While leaving the place I knew and loved so well was difficult, God didn't leave me alone. He not only gave me an incredible opportunity to keep coaching and developing young men at Tennessee, but He also blessed me to continue in my passion and pursue new opportunities to help in the community in other ways, along with a host of new friends who would deeply affect my life.

Enter Jim Haslam.

My friendship with Mr. Haslam began through a mutual friend, Don Evans. Don had served as the Secretary of Commerce for President George W. Bush, as well as the Chairman of the Board at the University of Texas when they hired me. Over the years, Don had become like a brother to me, and I had grown to trust him completely. So when Don told me I needed to get on the phone with a dear friend of his—somebody, he claimed, I would absolutely love—I paid close attention. Don told me that no one loves the state of Tennessee—and the University of Tennessee—more than this gentleman. He said that I *had* to meet Jim Haslam.

Don Evans drove us from our final press conference at Texas to the airport where one of Mr. Haslam's jets sat idling for me and my wife, Candy. How fitting that Mr. Haslam's plane would transport us to the blessings of the next chapter of our lives in Tennessee. Little did I know how much his character and wisdom would continue to be such a huge part of the blessings in the days to come.

Once I had been in Tennessee for a little while, Mr. Haslam and I got together for lunch. When I sat down with him, I was surprised how much he knew about my background—and honestly, how much he knew about *me*. He was so kind and gracious, yet I knew there was no ulterior motive.

"I can tell you have a passion for kids," he said.

"You're right, Mr. Haslam. I do."

I had been looking for the best place to get involved in the community, but, being new to Knoxville, I wasn't sure where to start. Little did I know that I was sitting across from the man who knew more about serving the community than anyone on this planet. He directed me towards the Emerald Youth Foundation here in town, which does incredible work for children in our area, serving about three thousand kids a day. I followed his counsel and have since loved every minute of working with this organization and its talented leadership. But this wasn't the last time Mr. Haslam would enrich my life.

Every time I'm on the road and I can stop at a Pilot, I always call Mr. Haslam to let him know that I have just left whatever store I've visited. He always asks me about the quality of the service and the cleanliness of the bathrooms ... and so far, I have been able to tell him that every one of his travel centers has been a thumbs-up experience. I'm not surprised because they reflect his character and excellence.

I don't know if I've ever met a more generous, kind, and loving person than Mr. Haslam. I also doubt I could name two or three athletes who have gone on to do as much good for their universities. Don Evans was right: no one loves the state of Tennessee or the University of Tennessee more than Jim Haslam.

He has a willingness to invest so much more than just money in community endeavors. If you have the means, it is easy to give money, but Mr. Haslam also gives his time, which is the greatest gift you can offer anyone. He would agree that he's been blessed financially and it is all too easy for people to focus on this aspect of his life. But when you really get to know him, you'll discover that giving money is only a small part of his philanthropy. The more impactful element of his life is that he is a generous, heartfelt giver of his very self, not just his resources.

My time with Mr. Haslam has proven to me that he is also one of the most positive people I've ever been around. I once went with him to a Cleveland Browns game during a time when they were struggling as a team. Throughout the whole experience, Mr. Haslam remained genuinely positive, insisting that if they just would keep working hard, everything would be fine. He wasn't putting on airs; he meant every word.

His positivity has also affected our basketball program. Our first few years in Knoxville were spent trying to build a strong foundation for the future, which meant we always didn't achieve the best record on the floor. Times were tough, but Mr. Haslam called me after almost every game. He still does. He leaves wonderful messages on my phone that encourage me, but also build up my guys. His wonderfully sweet and brilliant wife, Natalie (the bigger basketball fan in the family), is always in the background sharing her own encouragements as well. We actually live on the same street in Knoxville, so when I see them pulling out of the driveway, we often stop to talk. They are always just as gracious and encouraging in person.

Mr. Haslam has never been critical of our program, not even once. Instead, he always lets me know that he appreciates what we're doing, even after a tough loss. I keep most of these voicemails on my phone because his and Natalie's words are such an encouragement to me.

He is not *just* an optimist, however—though he certainly is one. His heart is to always put other people first, which also makes him a leader that people want to follow. Knowing a little about his history in the military and business, I have no doubt that if something difficult needs to be done, he will be the first one to do it. I don't think he would ever ask you to do something that he hasn't done or wouldn't do himself.

I call this simple, selfless leadership.

In fact, I am sometimes bothered when Mr. Haslam gets criticized in the media for things that, quite frankly, he hasn't done. He is so generous and influential that his name is associated with many organizations and endeavors. However, any hairbrained idea suggesting that he's running this university is completely ridiculous. Since I have known him, he has never stuck his nose into any situation without someone inviting him to offer his opinion or counsel. He'll tell you what he thinks—and what he thinks is something you should listen to—but he is not one of those egotistical guys who has to run the show. Nothing could be further from the truth.

One of my funniest memories involves Mr. Haslam and former President George W. Bush. It is no secret that after he left office, the President took up painting as a serious hobby. Don Evans informed me that the President had painted a special piece of art as a gift for Mr.

Haslam, one that featured Smokey, the bluetick hound that serves as Tennessee's unofficial mascot.

Knowing that Mr. Haslam and I live on the same street and often stop to chat, President Bush inquired about the possibly of shipping the painting to my house so I could deliver it to Mr. Haslam. In the end, they ended up delivering by another method. Regardless, as you can imagine, Mr. Haslam *loves* the painting. It still hangs in his house at Blackberry Farm.

Sometime later in 2018, Don Evans flew in from Texas to watch us play Georgia. A win in this game meant that we would secure the regular season SEC Championship, which we did. It was a big moment. Don and I were hanging out after the game when President Bush called Don's phone so he could congratulate me on our victory. After talking for a few minutes, I said, "By the way, Mr. President, Mr. Haslam loves that picture of Smokey that you drew for him."

"Barnes, you redneck!" the President replied. "That's not a picture! That's a painting!"

I guess the President was right. I don't know much about art, but I do know an honorable man when I see him. I can truly say that Jim Haslam is a man of integrity, generosity, and honor. The tentacles of his influence have reached far and wide. Even so, he remains humble and unassuming, shying away when people want to talk about him. It is evident that he loves people, which is why I love *him* so much. Mr. Haslam is a giant among men—with a giant heart to prove it.

DOUG DICKEY

University of Tennessee Football Head Coach (1964–1969)
University of Tennesseee Athletic Director (1985–2002)

JIM HASLAM IS THE TYPE OF MAN EVERYONE WOULD WANT AS A friend. "His cup runneth over," but he has never exploited or wasted his efforts. Thousands upon thousands of people have benefited from his and Natalie's generosity. Those impacted by his influence range from local people to university people—and from people within Tennessee to people across the nation. His reach is far and wide.

He is, without a doubt, the most accomplished businessman and philanthropist in the history of Tennessee athletics—and probably in the history of all University of Tennessee graduates. Starting as a Team Captain, he has gone on to become a community leader and an extraordinary giver to various charitable causes. He was a senior member of the UT Board of Trustees and the Chairman of my athletic board for a long time. Over the years, he proved to be a trustworthy friend, one that I could always approach for advice and counsel.

Jim Haslam is a no-nonsense guy. However, he is also easy to talk to and a good listener. Around 1967, Jim and I launched out in business together. I had secured the franchise rights in East Tennessee for a restaurant chain called Minnie Pearl Chicken. We built the first Minnie Pearl Chicken restaurant next door to a Pilot station on Kingston Pike. It was a forward-thinking idea at the time; putting franchises inside or near service stations was something we were exploring before anyone else we knew. We had a great time with the endeavor. In the end, Minnie Pearl Chicken didn't make it, but Pilot certainly did.

When I first interviewed for the job of Athletic Director at Tennessee, Jim and another UT official flew down to Tampa to meet with me. I took them to lunch at the Mullet Inn, which offered smoked mullet as the house specialty. We had a great conversation. I ultimately took the job and served as the Athletic Director at the University of Tennessee

for eighteen years. During that time, I interacted with Jim on countless occasions as we endeavored together to support various projects,
which included building new facilities on campus. Over the years, we've
laughed many times about how rich a life we were living back then to
have the whole journey begin at the Mullet Inn.

Jim has remained a great friend to this day, and I always enjoy visiting
with him when we see each other. Again, I can't think of anyone who has
been more valuable to the history of the University of Tennessee than
Jim Haslam.

DR. JOE JOHNSON

University of Tennessee President (1990–1999)

JIM HASLAM, ALONG WITH HIS FAMILY AND HIS BUSINESS, SET THE standard in the Knoxville area for generous, private support of deserving programs and organizations for the benefit of the people of this part of the world.

Jim was open to gift requests as long as the person requesting a gift did not make their request last longer than fifteen to twenty minutes. Hence, when I called on Jim for a gift for the University of Tennessee, the UT Medical Center, Knox County Imagination Library, the Helen Ross McNabb Mental Health Center, the Museum of Appalachia, the Boy Scouts, or other organizations, I had to be prepared to present the case for the gift in short order. Jim would give a carefully considered response to the gift request.

Jim not only *made* gifts for himself, his family, his foundation, and Pilot Company, he also *sought* gifts from other people and foundations in our community. Jim is a generous donor, and he is an exemplary fundraiser for deserving programs and organizations. The late Mr. Lindsay Young once said he would rather receive a call from the IRS than a call from Jim Haslam! He was that effective at separating you from your money, even though it was always for the most worthy of causes.

When Knoxville-area organizations considered private fundraising efforts, their leaders often sought Jim's wise counsel. He has a remarkable understanding of our community and the interests and passions of the people who will determine the response to a particular private gifts campaign. In fact, a gift from Jim would send an important message to other possible donors.

The impact of the gifts Jim Haslam, Natalie Haslam, the Haslam family, and Pilot Company have made to the University of Tennessee is transformational. Jim and his family understand well how significant private gifts can enhance the quality and scope of academic and athletic programs. The Haslam College of Business and the UT School of Music vividly demonstrate the beneficial impact of some sizeable gifts. All of us involved with the University of Tennessee appreciate more than we can say the willingness of Jim and Natalie to listen to requests for major gifts, to consider them, and to make them. The results are better students, better faculty, better facilities, and better technology.

Jim Haslam is committed to the use of his fiscal well-being for the benefit of his University of Tennessee and his community and its people. A casual review of any deserving program or organization in Knoxville will turn up a Haslam-related gift, but his greatest contribution is his leadership gift.

LAMAR ALEXANDER
United States Senator

It may seem presumptuous, but when I found out Jim Haslam was writing a book, I thought of the perfect title: *Football, Bathrooms, and Birthdays: The Story of Big Jim Haslam.*

Most people are already familiar with his experiences in football, but you may not know that when Jim started Pilot, he would visit every one of his stores regularly. When he did, the first place he would always check was the bathroom, just to make sure it was clean. Caring deeply about details has always been his leadership style—and he has kept it up even when Pilot continued to grow to hundreds of locations. If a Pilot bathroom is dirty, the manager may very well hear about it directly from the top.

Concerning birthdays, I know as recently as the age of eighty-seven, he took several hours in the mornings—even on vacation, mind you— to call every Pilot team member who had a birthday that day to wish them well. This is just the kind of person and leader he is—and he has been a great friend to me for many years.

I have always taken special note of the easy relationship he has with his family. When Governor Bill Haslam was delivering his inaugural address, he was obviously comfortable being Jim Haslam's son. There is no doubt he had been afforded many advantages when he was young, but he wasn't hung up on that. Many sons and daughters of high-profile people struggle with this, but you could tell Bill was comfortable with it—and also grateful for it. The fact that he was born on first or second base seemed to empower him with even more incentive to try to get home on his own so he could make his dad proud of him.

This is a real tribute to Jim and his family: they raise their kids and grandchildren in an environment where they're clearly fortunate financially, but they still work hard. They are taught to respect other people and respect their parents in the way most parents would desire and admire. I know that last Thanksgiving, the Haslams had sixty-five family members in attendance for dinner, fifteen of them great-grandchildren. Gathering as such an enormous group reflects the high value placed on family in the Haslam household.

My first memory of Jim is when I was ten years old and growing up in Maryville, just south of Knoxville. We were big UT football fans, so much so that that on Saturday afternoons during games everybody had their radios turned up so loud that when you walked up our street, you could hear the play-by-play announcer. Jim was Captain of the UT football team, and they were playing in the 1951 Cotton Bowl. This was the year they became National Champions. They won that game against Texas by a score of 20–14. It was an incredible season and it made an impression on me. Growing up in Maryville, Tennessee, I knew well the name Jim Haslam, as well as the names of guys like Doug Atkins, Hank Lauricella, and Johnny Majors.

I first met him in 1966 when I was a volunteer for Howard Baker's campaign. I had recently graduated from law school, after which I lived for a year in New Orleans clerking for Judge Wisdom. I had volunteered to work in Howard Baker's Senate campaign, but I never heard back from him. Thus, when I came home for Easter, I went to see him in person.

I assumed Howard Baker's organization would be large and organized. After all, his parents had both been members of Congress, and Baker was a well-known name in politics. But when I met him in his Knoxville law office, only he and Hugh Branson were around. It was underwhelming for sure. He then sent me over to his campaign offices, where his staff consisted of Ruthie Edmondson at the front desk, Bill Hamby smoking cigarettes in the back room, and a terrible clacking noise coming from one of the other rooms, which was Victor Ashe, home on spring break from Yale, typing out press releases. That was the entire Baker campaign team.

However, I also soon met volunteers like Jim Haslam, Bob Campbell, and George Morton. They were young and new to politics, getting their first taste of the process since we didn't have a statewide Republican party at the time. They helped in 1964 when he ran the first time, but Howard wouldn't be elected until 1966. Of course, Jim had only started his company a few years before, so he didn't yet have a lot of money. This didn't matter; he was already passionate and talented in raising money for the right causes even then.

We were all political neophytes, but these campaigns were how we got to know one another and become good friends. Jim and I have both talked about how the greatest thing about political participation is that it gives you a chance to meet people you would never meet otherwise. It throws all the balls up in the air, and they come down in unexpected places. If I had not volunteered for Howard Baker, I would have never met Jim Haslam.

In 1974, I was thirty-three years old and had secured the Republican nomination for Governor. However, this was the year of Watergate, a bad year for Republicans in general, and I lost the general election. Jim had helped me raise money during the campaign.

After I lost the election, most people thought this was the end of my political career, but Jim Haslam wouldn't hear of it. In early 1976, he hosted a fundraiser to help me pay off my campaign debt. Howard Baker attended and told the crowd, "Republicans have a bad habit of leaving our wounded lying on the field and left for dead. We don't want to do that for Lamar."

Jim and Natalie Haslam had barely finished their honeymoon. They flew back to their home in Knoxville and pulled off a successful fundraiser to help me reduce my debt. This was my introduction to Jim's constant participation in helping other people get elected to public office.

In 1978, Sandy Beall and I bought Blackberry Farm, which sounds like a big deal today, but it wasn't back then. At the time, it was rundown and ragged with bushes growing through the windows.

We purchased it from the estate of Howard Jarvis for $110,000 (almost all of it borrowed) with three goals in mind. The first goal was that Sandy and his wife, Kreis, and my wife, Honey, and I wanted to have a cabin for ourselves and our families. Secondly, Sandy and Kreis wanted to turn it into a nice inn. Lastly, we wanted to protect as much land as possible on the Chilhowee Mountain from inappropriate development. We wanted future citizens to continue to have a natural view of the Smokies as they drove through the Townsend entrance to the mountains.

When we bought Blackberry Farm, we were able to secure options on several thousand acres of additional land in and around it, which was only about thirty acres itself. Although the price of that optioned land was only $300 or $400 an acre, Sandy and I didn't have any money. So we went to Jim Haslam.

He and Natalie came and looked at what we were doing. After some conversation, they became our partners, and we optioned the land in 1978. For the next 20 years, we split the cost and sent the sellers monthly checks to pay for it. Since then, along with a few other families, we've continued to buy land, selling off four or five lots with each tract to pay for it. We then donated the rest of the land to create conservation easements that can never be developed.

So since 1978, Jim has been our partner in creating conservation easements on several thousand acres of land along several miles of the Chilhowee Mountain Ridge at the Walland and Townsend entrances to the Smokies so the view and ecology of these priceless landscapes will be forever protected. Most people don't know that he has had any role in this, but he gives Natalie credit for making him an environmentalist; after all, she encouraged him to do it.

In 1978, I also asked him to be the Finance Chairman for my second race for Governor. From my first race, I had learned that a lot of people who give money expect something in return. They don't always say it, but particularly with a job like Governor where there are thirty-eight thousand employees and you spend billions of dollars every year, there can be quite the expectation.

I asked Jim Haslam to be my Chairman because he didn't want anything. There was nothing I could do for him that he couldn't already do for himself. I told him I wanted to put someone between me and everyone else—someone who didn't have an angle to gain something from the role. He did this very well for me, so much so that he also served as my Finance Chairman for my third Governor's race in 1982 and in all three of the Senate races I've won since that time.

While I was Governor, Jim only ever asked me for two things, one of which I vetoed and the other I opposed. The first request was that I would sign a bill allowing liquor to be sold by the drink at the Knoxville airport during the 1982 World's Fair. I told him I was going to veto the bill because the airport was in Blount County, and the county government had passed a resolution opposing liquor by the drink. At that time, whether to sell liquor by the drink was, by law, a county option decision, and I felt I had to respect the county's decision. The second issue was when we successfully passed a law limiting billboards in Tennessee—and since Pilot had billboards everywhere, Jim was not a fan and didn't want us to pass such legislation. Thus, he loves to joke with me that during the eight years when I was Governor, I vetoed and opposed the only two things he ever wanted from me.

So many people in Knoxville and East Tennessee ask Jim Haslam for something every hour of the day. One of his greatest characteristics is that he always says, "We'll work it out." He is the most generous person I know. However, he's also very intentional about his generosity, especially for the University of Tennessee.

When I was University President, Jim, Natalie, Jimmy, and Dee would often talk to me about the ways their money could be best used at the university. They didn't just give it; they gave it *carefully*, especially in Jim's case for the School of Business, and in Natalie's case for the School of Music.

I had the chance to be a part of something special for the College of Music. My son, Drew, came across the original lead sheet for the famous song "The Tennessee Waltz," national anthem of country music. We knew we had to acquire it, so four of us (Steve Smith, Lew Conner, Ted Welsh, and myself), along with our spouses, bought the original lead sheet. The song was the work of two songwriters, Peewee King and Red Stewart, who wrote it one night just after World War II while driving from Memphis to Nashville. They put the music on a page, and the next day they took it to their publisher, Wesley Rose, and the rest is history. At any rate, we bought it and presented it to Natalie. That original lead sheet is now displayed in the Natalie Haslam School of Music on campus.

Jim and Natalie have also created scholarships and professorships to support the university in the endeavors that will help the most. They receive a lot of publicity for their participation with athletics. However, I'm confident that they are more generous with the academic side of the university than with athletics. This is what happens when you care deeply for a certain place, which is evident by the fact that Jim was a terrific member of the UT Board of Trustees.

It is also no secret that Jim is a tremendously effective fundraiser. I think one reason this is true is because he is so generous himself, so when he calls other people, they have to be responsive to him. He is just such a good example that it is hard not to follow him. One afternoon in August 2014 during my campaign for re-election to the United States Senate, I sat with him by the telephone and, in about two hours, watched him raise $700,000 for my general election effort. I've never met anyone as enthusiastic and effective at raising money.

Personally, Jim is so enthusiastic that he's *noisy*. If he is at a restaurant having dinner, you'll know he's there because he has such a big laugh booming through such a big voice. One of his best friends, Ross Faires, who has since passed away, once played a prank on him. Jim and Natalie were in Nantucket, where they rented a home every summer. Ross called the house and disguised his voice, telling them he was a representative of the Nantucket Anti-Noise Committee. He told them that they had received numerous complaints about the noise at the Haslam residence, so they needed to tone it down. It took a long time for Jim to figure out it was Ross.

I love that Jim Haslam can be heard. After all, his life and the way he has lived it has so much to teach us all. I am not only grateful for his friendship, I am proud of it.

BOB CAMPBELL

College Friend & Fraternity Brother
Attorney for Pilot Company

THE FIRST GLIMPSE I HAD OF JIM HASLAM WAS IN THE FALL OF 1948 in a mathematics class we were both taking at the University of Tennessee. We were both freshmen at the time. Jim was a baby-faced young man who kept trying to answer all the questions. It was as if he were the only one the professor was actually teaching. I finally asked somebody else in the class, "Who is this guy who keeps answering all the questions?"

"He's a freshman football player," they replied. That was my first impression of Jim Haslam. It wouldn't be the last.

Later that semester, this guy became my fraternity brother, which meant we began spending a lot of time together. Quickly, we became great friends. As a football player, he was always hungry. We spent a lot of time in the fraternity house, but at night, we would often go to a diner down on the strip in the middle of campus, usually at about 10:00 p.m. Jim would always order a sweet roll with five dips of chocolate ice cream.

Over the decades since those wonderful nighttime snacks, Jim's life has changed and he has become more prosperous. He traded sweet rolls and ice cream for French petit fours and his smelly sneakers for Italian footwear. In terms of these temporal things, a change definitely occurred; but in terms of the man that he is, nothing has changed.

Because he has been so successful, some people might see Jim as aloof or above others, but I've never known a person who has been more down to earth or concerned with serving others. I've also never met a man more loyal to his family, friends, fraternity brothers, and teammates, and this continues up to the present day, some seventy years later.

The name Jim Haslam is synonymous with total loyalty.

Jim tragically lost his wife, Cynthia, in an uncommonly early fashion. A while later, he began dating Natalie. Their first public date was to a Tennessee football game in the fall of 1975. He invited me and my wife,

Ruth, to go with them to the game. Back then, Jim would usually sit in the main part of the stadium until halftime, at which time he would walk out into the concourse to meet up with all his old football buddies. They would talk about the game until halftime was over. But during this particular game, he never left his seat. He was just so terribly nervous to be dating again—especially in public. However, his nerves continued even after the game was over. This was the infamous night that he grabbed a head of cabbage instead of the head of lettuce.

I have had the honor of being more than just friends with Jim; I have also been his attorney for many years. Back when we were in school, I was working toward my undergraduate degree, but I didn't know what I wanted to do. All I knew was that I didn't want to be an engineer, scientist, or accountant. One day while we were sitting in the diner down on the strip, I decided that I wanted to go to law school. Back in those days, you didn't have to take an LSAT or go through any preliminary examinations, so I literally just walked across the street and signed up for law school.

After I graduated and passed the bar exam, I had a license to practice law, but I had no clients, no prospects, and consequently, no money. I was as green as I could be, but in 1958, Jim believed in me enough to ask me to help him form Pilot Oil Corporation. Having such a great opportunity at this particular time in my life was a godsend because it gave me a client. But more importantly, it gave me the continuation of what would be a lifetime friendship with Jim Haslam and his family.

When the corporation was formed, Jim decided the ownership of the company would never be in the hands of any entity or individual other than someone named Haslam. Even this early, he already had quite a clear vision about keeping the company on the right track. Over the years, I have often laughed to myself about the fact that the average guy on the street probably doesn't realize just how smart and perceptive Jim Haslam is—and he has been this way since he was young. I used to joke with him that *he* was actually the general counsel for Pilot Oil

Corporation because he was smart enough to know the answer to a lot of questions.

This also meant he did a lot of things on his own, which sometimes gave his lawyer more than a few gray hairs. On more than one occasion, I can remember Jim calling me at home or at the office to tell me about a contract he wanted me to review, just to see if it was okay. I would say, "Okay, Jim, I'll be glad to do it. When do you need it?" He would reply, "Well, I signed it yesterday." He was just that aggressive and efficient—and, most of the time, his intuition was spot on.

The good thing about having Jim as your client was that no matter how much he might forge ahead, he always did so with integrity. I don't recall the specifics of the situation, but I do remember a moment early in my representation of Pilot when there was a certain transaction being negotiated and the typical questions of such a circumstance were being hashed out. As is the case with these kinds of things questions were being asked that could have multiple answers, depending upon the context. Concerning one of these questions, Jim asked me how he should answer. I said, "Let me make a suggestion: just answer it by telling the truth."

That made perfect sense to him because he was a man who had already bought into being honest with every fiber of his being, not only in his business practices but also in life in general. He has always endeavored to tell the truth, even if it hurts, simply because it is the right thing to do. Being consistent with his principles of honesty and integrity is so much more important to him than being successful.

I was also involved in Jim's entry into the political arena. In 1964, a young lawyer from Harriman, Tennessee, named Frank Qualls was running for Congress against John Duncan, the Mayor of Knoxville at the time. I nudged Jim to help with Qualls's campaign because I knew that, even at this early stage of his career, he had an uncanny ability to raise money. He got involved but didn't finish the full campaign because he became a little concerned about opposing the Mayor of Knoxville at that particular time, mainly because he was so heavily involved in so many other civic matters in the city. As always, his concern was for the welfare of Knoxville.

In 1976, we were both delegates to the Republican National Convention. President Gerald Ford was running against Ronald Reagan. Jim and I were both delegates for Ford, and the convention was being held in Kansas City. We stayed in the same hotel with Howard Baker, who was the leader of the Senate Republican Conference at the time. Senator Baker was also supporting President Ford.

The whole convention—including the media and delegates gathered at our hotel—was abuzz with rumors that President Ford would ask Howard Baker to be his Vice Presidential running mate. He seemed to be a logical choice. Everyone was scurrying about waiting for the official announcement, but then suddenly all the crowds vanished. We soon found out that President Ford had called Senator Baker to inform him that he was asking Bob Dole to be his running mate instead.

If you know Jim Haslam, then you know he loved Howard Baker. This news was quite disappointing, but, as should be expected with Jim, it did not affect Jim's involvement over a good part of his adult life in the support of Howard Baker. This connection sometimes brought me into interesting places with Jim, including being in Washington, D.C., and attending some of the Watergate committee meetings, which was certainly historically significant at that particular time.

Besides his faith, family, and friends, Jim Haslam's greatest passions are the University of Tennessee and the community of Knoxville. No one is surprised by the fact that Jim is considered to be the best fundraiser for worthy causes in the history of Knoxville. We all know about the public campaigns for Boys and Girls Clubs, United Way, and many more well-known organizations, but nobody really knows (I have some idea) how many smaller, seemingly less significant things Jim Haslam supports and champions. If there is any worthwhile cause, he will listen carefully and consider its support. There is no doubt in my mind that the Knoxville community would be nowhere near what it is today if it was not for Jim Haslam. I think most people would agree with me.

He is still so very loyal—like family—to his old teammates, even though not many of them are left. The ones who are still here are very close to Jim. The same rings true for his fraternity brothers. He's a remarkable guy because he's never changed—and none of this is staged. I have no pride in authoring this excerpt, but I do have tremendous pride in having Jim as a friend for seventy-two years and counting. Even though he has been so prosperous and achieved a status that few people will ever reach, he is still the same old Jim Haslam of the sweet rolls and five dips of chocolate ice cream. He's Jim Haslam, my friend.

JIMMY SMITH

College Friend & Fraternity Brother
Former Member of Pilot Company Board of Directors

Jim Haslam came to Knoxville on a train, but nobody met him at the station. It was nighttime, so he walked over to the stadium looking for his assigned room. The rooms were curiously numbered and, when he found what he thought was his room, he encountered a much older, hard-nosed, extremely hairy football player he assumed was his roommate... it was not. In fact, we're still not sure who it was.

Regardless, the young man must have thought, *What have I done?* But he went back and checked the room number again to discover he was on the wrong floor and this much older man was not his roommate. Needless to say, he didn't have a very warm welcome the first day he arrived in Knoxville.

That year, I was the rush Chairman of Sigma Chi, and we began having contact with him. He was a year behind me in school, but he had developed good relationships with several other guys from our fraternity. To make a long story short, he soon became a Sigma Chi along with the rest of us.

He had an innocent, young-looking face, which was why he was given the nickname *Youngin'*. He was 6' 4" inches tall and weighed about two hundred pounds, which was very big in those days. Despite his physique, he was an open, non-antagonistic, non-confrontational type of person. There was nothing dark or conniving about him, not in the least.

People liked him, so much so that within just a few weeks of being at the University of Tennessee, he had developed a lot of relationships. Most of those relationships continued throughout their respective lifetimes, though most of our classmates from those days are now deceased. Jim was just a good, open, innocent kind of person, so the affectionate nickname *Youngin'* just fit him well.

After college, most everyone went into the Army. As an ROTC Second Lieutenant, Jim was called to active duty and sent to Korea with the engineers. Even though he was only a Second Lieutenant, he became a Company Commander. When he returned home, he didn't know what he was going to do. Then along came a man named Sam Claiborne, who, besides General Robert R. Neyland, became one of the main influences in his life. Sam worked in the cut-rate gasoline business, which introduced Jim to the concept of achieving volume by selling at the lowest price. This is why Pilot has always been a low-cost operator.

I can remember the days when Pilot had a board up on the wall that would show how many gallons they sold that day, including the margins and the total expenses per gallon. From the beginning, they've always been able to compete on prices.

After starting a company called Sail Oil and then selling his share to Sam Claiborne, Jim was able to make enough money to create Pilot Oil in 1958. He started the company on his dining room table at his house on Scenic Drive. The table took a beating when his first employee, Jim Shelby, dropped an adding machine on it. Shelby survived the ordeal, as did Pilot. I was not there on the first day, but arrived on the third day or so. In those early days. I was mainly just a friend and a kibitzer—and not involved in the company in any way.

The whole secret to the business was finding good locations to open up new stations. You had to convince an owner to either rent or sell his or her property. Jim Haslam has two significant qualities that have served him well in this endeavor: high energy and unlimited optimism. Add the fact that he has also always been a hard worker, success was simply bound to come to him.

Jim would start early in the morning and keep going all day long. Often, he would be out scouting new locations and spend the night wherever he was traveling in Virginia, West Virginia, Georgia, South Carolina, North Carolina, Kentucky, or Tennessee. He was persistent in pursuing and acquiring these locations. It might take him six months to acquire a location, but if he found the right property, he would just keep talking to the owner until he eventually convinced him into renting or selling. Jim Haslam's persistence and determination have always been the secret behind Pilot's growth.

One day, Jim invited me to ride with him to Louisville, Kentucky, where I was registered to attend a conference. We started about 8:00 a.m. and went first to Corbin, Kentucky, to visit his station there. We then drove over to Danville where he was looking at prospective sites. Next we went to Lexington. At about 4:00 p.m., we finally arrived in Louisville.

We didn't check into a motel. Instead, he just began driving around looking at traffic patterns and trying to determine what properties might be the best in the area. We finally checked into a motel about 6:00 p.m. and had supper. Afterward, we went out and started doing the same thing again, just driving around and looking at different locations. We finally came back and went to bed around 10:00 p.m. The next morning at 6:00 a.m., he was up and running at the same pace doing the same thing again—and could do this day after day with seemingly no loss of energy.

There is no doubt that he has always had good judgment and made great decisions, but to me, the main factors have always been his energy and positive thinking. We used to go to UT football games and all gather in the concourse at halftime. Even if Tennessee was down by twenty points, Jim Haslam would think that we were still going to win.

Compared to Jim Haslam, I've always tried to be more realistic. It took me a long time to appreciate the fact that he did not tolerate negative thinking. Failure isn't in his vocabulary. He was very knowledgeable and had good judgment—and he always tried to have a place to safely land.

We worked together on various boards. I was on the Board of Directors at Pilot. My family owned a meatpacking company at one time, and Jim served on its Board of Directors. He also became a Director of three banks, including two where I was the CEO.

Later, our families did a lot together. For three summers, we went with them to Jekyll Island, where we had houses just down the beach from each other. All our kids and families would engage in athletic contests—football, baseball, or anything we could have fun competing at. We've also gone on a lot of other vacations together as well, often with other couples. We've been to Australia, Africa, New Zealand, Europe, and South America.

Jim and I still talk a lot, mostly about the Cleveland Browns, but also about business in general. He is the godfather to our oldest daughter, Janet, and my wife and I are godparents to his son Bill. All told, my life has been enriched in countless ways by the many, many years of friendship with Jim Haslam.

DAN MATHEWS

Rector, St. John's Cathedral (1972–1980)

IN THE SUMMER OF 1972, MY WIFE, DEENER, AND I HAD JUST FINISHED construction of our mountaintop retreat called The Swag near Waynesville, North Carolina. The long and rather steep road up the side of the mountain was an engineering challenge and considered by our mountain neighbors to be impossible to ever construct.

Jim Haslam, Senior Warden at St. John's, had been given my name by Bishop Sanders to possibly be a priest in the Diocese of Tennessee. Jim's popular Rector, Frank Cerveny, had left St. John's Knoxville to serve the Cathedral in Jacksonville, Florida. Eager to take charge of the calling process, Jim drove over to his Pilot Oil Station in Maggie Valley, North Carolina, and asked his manager, "Where is The Swag?"

Before answering, his manager glanced out the window and drawled, "Mr. Haslam, there ain't no way you gonna get that Cadillac up that mountain." Yet up he came and, as a result of our mountaintop interview, Deener and I moved from St. David's Church in Nashville to become Jim's new Rector of St. John's in downtown Knoxville.

During an interview that followed sometime later in a Knoxville restaurant near the Pilot headquarters, Jim spotted a group of his employees. As we were getting up to leave, Jim greeted them with a few warm wishes and laughter, then discreetly picked up their check and paid it with mine as we left. I thought to myself, *Wow, this is the kind of generous-hearted church layman with whom I would like to serve as Pastor and Rector.*

Having left a suburban church in Nashville in the West Meade section of that city, my experience in the ministry had been limited to a well-defined neighborhood of young couples and children. With this move to Knoxville and a much more varied downtown church I was unfamiliar with, it was not long before an unhappy parishioner called and complained bitterly about something I had done as the new and inexperienced Rector. I called Jim immediately to ask for his advice. His words were clear and simple, "Whenever you get a complaint, call me first, and I will tell you whether you need to worry about it." In those first few years, he got plenty of calls from me and the practical wisdom for which he is known was always on target.

I was honored and privileged to preach the funeral for Jim's wife, Cynthia. Her sudden death was a shock to the whole state, as well as to the family. My relationship with Jim grew deeply during those difficult months of grief. When he began dating Natalie Tucker, I informed him that the church had certain regulations and rules about marriage. He followed those canonical procedures with care and, after the prescribed time, the Bishop gave me permission to marry them at St. John's in a glorious and sacred ceremony on February 28, 1976. What a special day that was to have Cynthia's best friend and Miss Tennessee fill the void in Jim's life as a result of his wife's passing. The bond between these two has grown deeper every year since I helped them tie the knot.

Bishop Sanders once promoted a program called Ventures in Mission. The goal was to raise $3 million across the diocese, and he asked me if I would serve as chair. My answer to the Bishop was, "Only if I could be Jim Haslam's co-chair." At our first meeting, Jim looked across his desk at me and said, "Okay, Dan, how much are you and Deener going to pledge?" I thought, *This was supposed to be about other people giving, but now Haslam had made it about my giving!* I stumbled for a figure and after I blurted it out, he quickly said, "Well, you can give that over three years." Then on his yellow note pad he wrote three times my original pledge.

It was then and there that I learned why he is Knoxville's premier fundraiser. Then he wrote on the next line of his yellow pad, "Natalie and Jim Haslam $100,000." I witnessed most definitively not only his fund-raising prowess but also his enormous generosity as well. We raised the three million dollars, but not without flying in his private plane through storms, snow, and turbulence like I had never before experienced. During these turbulent times, I struggled with nausea . . . while Jim was eating his sandwich and drinking a Tab. How grateful I was when the Venture in Mission travel ended for me and the diocese celebrated its financial victory.

Since leaving my role as Jim and Natalie's St. John's Rector and eventually serving at Trinity Church Wall Street, Deener and I still treasure our visits with the Haslams in their home. On one such recent visit, they asked if we would like to join them at a UT basketball game. We were delighted to discover that their seats were right on the floor in the very first row. The energy, noise, and excitement right in front of us was almost overwhelming. Cheerleaders jumped up and down a few feet in front of our knees and the big, tall players were only an arm's length away. A ball headed out of bounds flew right over my head. A visiting player attempting to grab it, lost his balance, and fell straight over me! I landed on my back with the player completely covering me up. With the crushed, broken chair beneath me, all I could hear was Jim Haslam's voice yelling at the referee, "It's our ball! It's our ball!" This competitive core of Jim Haslam, the athlete, trumped any concern for the well-being of his former Rector, flattened on the floor next to him.

Nothing in Jim Haslam's life is more important than his three remarkable children and Natalie's three esteemed daughters, along with all of their spouses and children. His granddaughter spent her honeymoon at the same Swag where Jim and I first met. In 2018, forty-six years after we met, she and her husband bought the Swag Resort; thus the Haslam "touch" continues to this third generation.

The stories are endless. It is hard to be around Jim Haslam without something memorable happening. When God created him, He made a most unusually gifted, brilliant, and energized soul to bring blessings to the rest of us—and Jim has done this successfully his entire life.

BILL BARRON

Pastor of Sequoyah Hills Presbyterian Church (1985–2008)
Founder of Ministry of the Laity

JIM HASLAM AND I KNEW EACH OTHER FROM A DISTANCE IN THE 1980s. I was a friend of his priest, the Very Reverend James L. Sanders, Dean of St. John's Cathedral, who had moved to Knoxville a year before I was called to Sequoyah Hills Presbyterian Church. Jim Sanders became my priest in some respects, and on one occasion he asked if I knew the Haslams.

He said that he'd like to connect us, but the timing wasn't right with our full plates of responsibilities. Jim Sanders was not a man of lavish praise, but he lauded Jim and Natalie Haslam for what I recall as a couple of hours. I later learned through my own encounters that he had not exaggerated a word! The relationship between the Sanders and the Haslams was extraordinary, even beyond Jim's position at St. John's and after moving from Knoxville. These couples loved and adored each other.

Years later, the Haslams attended a memorial service I officiated for one of our mutual friends. After the service, Mr. Haslam sent a memorial contribution to our church with a personal note. It read, "If there is ever anything I can do for you, please let me know."

Twelve years ago I contacted him and asked for his counsel about options in retirement. He was consumed at that point with his son's gubernatorial campaign, but soon after Bill Haslam was elected Governor, Jim contacted me, just as he promised. His wise counsel resulted in a community ministry that lasted almost ten years, sponsored by him, Tommy Ayres, Bo Shafer, and Wayne Ritchie. Jim and Natalie's regular participation in this ministry encouraged others to make the commitment and enriched our weekly experiences. Our relationship quickly developed into a friendship that my wife, Eleanor, and I have cherished since.

About ten years ago, our phone rang on Thanksgiving morning. It was the Haslams. I suspect they call a lot of people with the same message, but it was one we treasure! Their message was, "On this Thanksgiving Day, we wanted to let you know we are thankful to God for the Barrons." It was a remarkable and humbling gift of validation. We still shake our heads in astonishment that, with as many relationships and responsibilities as they had, they took the time and cared enough to call us.

Adjectives are inadequate to describe the qualities and actions of the Haslams and all they mean to our community. It's not only the financial support that they and Pilot Company give to almost every worthwhile endeavor in Knoxville; it's also their personal compassion and unconditional generosity extended to friends from all over the city, given without fanfare. Their love of Knoxville and the University of Tennessee is evidenced by their fingerprints across the city.

Jim is a man of humility, generosity, integrity, and encouragement. He listens intently and gives great advice. Natalie and Jim are examples of a rare team whose huge success is undergirded by their faith, friendships, love for St. John's Episcopal Cathedral, and their Savior and Lord, Jesus Christ. They are the epitome of grace and truth. How blessed I have been for that memorial note that invited me to let Mr. Haslam know if there was ever anything he could do for me! Thanks be to God!

JOHN ROSS

Dean of St. John's Cathedral (1996–Present)

JIM HASLAM HAS BEEN A PRESENCE IN MY LIFE SINCE 1985. WE'VE interacted more times than I can count, both professionally and personally. We've shared formal occasions, and we've shared private dinners. We've talked at parties, in business meetings, and even in hospital rooms during visits with recovering family members. Wherever and however we've crossed paths, Jim has always been the same Jim: thoughtful, engaging, warm, positive, personal, and present. He is a gentleman in the best sense. He is respectful of the people around him and is never too busy or too involved to be polite and respectful.

Jim is always the glass-half-full person. He makes decisions and moves forward decisively. Jim is quick to support a cause or offer a donation, almost exclusively without personal recognition. His generosity affects an amazing array of efforts—from a monetary gift to start the International Baccalaureate program at a local high school, to a substantial annual gift to allow clergy to play Santa for those in need.

In addition to financial gifts, Jim has a lot of advice to offer. I have been the recipient of many of his pearls of wisdom. Let me share a few vignettes …

Jim was the senior layperson at St. John's when I moved from my position as Sub-Dean to becoming the Dean (Senior Pastor). My first day, Jim took me to lunch at Naples and, after a bit of idle chatting (and well before our lunch was served), Jim asked if I knew the two most important things I would do as the Dean. I said "No," so he proceeded to tell me. First, Jim said that the most important mark would be the people I hired. "Those people," he said, "will affect the parish both positively and negatively more than you will!"

Second, he said, "The only way to operate is with a solid plan, so before you take the plane up, you better have a good idea where you are going to land." Thankfully, lunch arrived. The conversation was a little overwhelming, but I soon realized that he was right on every point—and I have practiced his pearls of wisdom throughout my ministry.

At another lunch during my early years, Jim asked, "Dean, do you know how you will know I am upset with you or with a decision you have made?"

"I don't think so, Jim."

"You'll know because I will give *more* money, not less." Sure enough, Jim has never withheld his generosity over a difference of opinion. He is always honest and always supportive because he believes—no, he knows—that the cause is more important than the leader.

Jim is funny. He is quick to laugh and loves humor. He loves the loud cymbal clanging on Easter morning. He wants a cymbal "played" at his funeral, a service that is to be short and also entail the taking up of a collection for the church. His instructions! I promised we would.

Whether at home or traveling, Jim and Natalie always attend church. They give the most and ask the least. Jim doesn't get caught up in debates over Christian doctrine, but reflects a simple faith God made us, all that God made is good, and God loves us. He puts those convictions into action. Jesus said, "To those who have been given much, much is required" (Luke 12:48). Jim would add that "much" should be returned to the community through our actions of charitable words and deeds.

Jim has given me the best gift of all: he taught me how to be generous. I am not sure I knew until I watched and listened to Jim. This small shift in my perspective shaped my ministry and life as much as any other learning or experience has.

Jim is the best.

WENDY HAMILTON

Pilot Team Member (1992–Present)

MY FIRST INTERACTION WITH MR. HASLAM WAS ON VALENTINE'S Day, 1992. At that time, Pilot was located in a very small office building off of Kingston Pike in Knoxville. I had only worked there about ten days when I found red roses on my desk.

As I looked around the office, I noticed all the women in the office had red roses on their desks. Mr. Haslam had purchased roses for all female team members for Valentine's Day. I was so thankful and wanted to tell him personally how grateful I was. Mr. Haslam and I had never met before that day, and he was so very welcoming and gracious. From that day on, I knew he was the kind of business leader and mentor I wanted in my life.

As my tenure with Pilot continued, I worked part-time and attended the University of Tennessee as a full-time student. I changed my degree from teaching to business because I wanted to work at Pilot after graduation. Mr. Haslam showed care and interest in my class schedule and my progress towards graduation. He always made a point to ask me about my classes and grades.

Through middle school and high school, my focus was on my social skills more than my education. I barely graduated high school, so when I graduated from UT with honors, my parents asked me what had changed. I told them that there was no way was I going to tell Jim Haslam that I was failing a class. They, too, were thankful for his influence in my life.

In his Letter to the Colossians, Paul says, "Therefore, as God's chosen people, holy and dearly loved, clothe yourselves with compassion, kindness, humility, gentleness and patience" (Colossians 3:12, NIV). This verse sums up the legacy Mr. Haslam has left in my life. He not only shows these things towards me; he exemplifies each of these characteristics in his daily interactions with everyone. He teaches us that a smile does not cost anything but can make a person's day, and it is better to have a good, positive attitude than a negative, complaining spirit.

One of my favorite things to hear is Mr. Haslam's laughter. His laughter alone makes everyone within earshot smile. God has blessed me with the example of Mr. Haslam in my life, and I am so thankful to Him for the opportunity to work for such a servant leader.

MEG COUNTS

Pilot Team Member (2015–Present)

MR. HASLAM HAS THE BEST LAUGH! IT CAN BE HEARD FROM A MILE away and could make anyone smile. He is the biggest family man, extremely close to all his children and his grandchildren and knowing everything about them. They are his life.

Mr. Haslam is the absolute *best* storyteller. He remembers everything and always has the best stories to tell about his family, life experiences, and the adventures of building the company. One of my earliest memories of Mr. Haslam was hearing his voice for the first time. All the Haslams have particularly loud and distinctive voices—in the best way. I have many memories of hearing Jimmy and Mr. Haslam talking and laughing. You could always tell they were very close.

Mr. Haslam means the world to all the team members at Pilot Company. He is beloved and respected by all and can light up any room in seconds. He has created a company where doing the right thing, working hard, taking care of our customers, showing kindness, and giving back are core foundations.

To Mr. Haslam, it is all about people. We often get companywide voicemails from him on many holidays ranging from Thanksgiving to Veterans Day, thanking team members for the work they do and acknowledging the special day. He also calls all the team members who work at the sales and support center in Knoxville on their birthdays, which is both amazing and an amazingly large task. He makes these calls in the mornings, and these voicemails become a treasure to all who receive them.

He is the definition of a servant leader. He has shown both the Pilot and Knoxville communities what servant leadership qualities really are and what someone can do when they apply them to every aspect of life. He has given his life to his family, country, and community in which he lives. In many ways, I don't know if Knoxville would be what it is today without Mr. Haslam and his leadership, his ability to inspire others, his capacity to see opportunities, and his stewardship.

BRAD MARTIN

Chairman and CEO of Proffit's/SAKS (1989–2007)
Member of Pilot Company Board of Directors

I FIRST MET MR. HASLAM THROUGH TENNESSEE POLITICS. I BECAME a member of the Tennessee House of Representatives at a young age. Early on, I learned Mr. Haslam was an established and respected leader in public policy and service. We would sometimes interact on various campaigns for candidates like Senator Baker, Governor and Senator Alexander, and Senator Corker. However, we worked much more closely when Bill Haslam ran for Governor.

My early recollection of him is that he was a very *large* figure in every sense of the term. Certainly, this was true of him from a physical standpoint, but it was also true of his presence, his energy, and his impact. He seemed to be more than just a person; he was a *force*.

After I left politics, I became involved with a department store called Proffit's, which was headquartered in Alcoa, Tennessee, just south of Knoxville. Over a handful of years, we acquired and grew the company, and I eventually became the CEO. Mr. Haslam and Jimmy had known me from politics, but now they knew me as someone involved in business in East Tennessee. One day, they invited me to breakfast at the Airport Hilton and asked if I would consider being on the Board of Directors for their family company, Pilot.

I was flattered by their request and hoped I could help a little bit, but I also knew I would learn a lot from them—and I was right. I was in a retail business; Pilot was an interstate retailer. I sold general merchandise, apparel, and home goods; Pilot sold petroleum products, food items, and other general merchandise. This role was definitely something different for me, but also a great opportunity to learn and contribute. This experience highlighted a characteristic I've always admired about Mr. Haslam—and one he has certainly imparted to Bill and Jimmy as well. He is constantly focused on learning and growing. Regardless of his success, he remains inquisitive and continually seeks out ways to make himself and his company better.

It takes an extraordinarily humble and growth-oriented person to think this way because, when you're the founder, CEO, and owner, it would be all too easy to stop seeking counsel from others, especially from those who don't know much about your business. It has always been evident that Mr. Haslam is a lifelong learner. He modeled this characteristic for me decades ago, and he continues to model it today.

Being in meetings with Mr. Haslam reveals his unique ability to ensure all the participants are focused on the most important topics. No matter how far into left field you might get, he always brings you back to the most critical things that should be discussed or worked on that moment. He is also a master at taking a topic that might be complicated and simplifying it in a manner that anyone can understand and act upon. This is a unique skill of a great leader, and I've seen him utilize it time and time again so everyone present could succeed in the task at hand.

During difficult problems or dark days, Mr. Haslam always gravitates to the optimistic side of things to find a solution or positive outcome. He is a trusted source of optimism for anyone who has the privilege of being around him. He's also tremendously grateful, which is something you can easily observe in his interactions with people. From cashiers to travel center team members to teachers in the community to members of the Board of Directors, Mr. Haslam never misses an opportunity to say, "Thank you for all you do!"

When you combine his incredible optimism and gratitude with his high-energy personality and generous spirit, the result is just enormous. It would take a lot of energy to chronicle the financial gifts Mr. Haslam and his family have provided to so many individuals, organizations, and important institutions, but he also utilizes the same level of generosity in the giving of his time, energy, optimism, insight, and gratitude. He does this no matter who or what it may be, whether pursuing a one-on-one relationship with a student receiving a scholarship or simply being involved with a certain cause or organization. Mr. Haslam puts his money where his heart is; in fact, he puts his entire *being* into these community initiatives.

When this combination of all that he is and all that he offers comes together to help others, it is truly powerful.

LEE SCOTT

President and CEO of Walmart (2000–2009)
Member of Pilot Company Board of Directors

My first meeting with Mr. Haslam—or Big Jim, as I call him—came at a White House Christmas dinner during the Bush administration. My wife was seated at one table, and I was seated at another next to a tall gentleman from Pilot Corporation, which I assumed was some kind of aviation company. It was not.

My father started out on Route 66 in southeast Kansas with one gas station. Many years later, he retired with two. Since it is in my family history, I've always had a natural interest and affinity for the business. Discovering that Big Jim owned over five hundred gas stations was quite an enjoyable experience that made me think about how different my family would be if we had opened this many gas stations. Needless to say, we had a great visit, and I really enjoyed our conversation together—but I had no idea I would ever have a real relationship with him or his company. I was just very impressed with the kind of person he was. It was evident he was the real deal.

Years later, Byron Trott and BDT Capital Partners made an investment in Pilot, and I was asked to be the observer on the board because of my association with Byron. Of course, this jogged my memory of Mr. Haslam and it remains such an interesting coincidence that I met him at the White House only to end up having a deeper connection with his company and his family.

As we began to work together, it became apparent to me that Big Jim had a uniquely positive outlook on life, business, and everything in between. However, I think there are times when a person is especially positive or has a great sense of humor that it becomes all too easy to miss the depth of that person, including his or her ability to lead and manage. He may be positive, but Big Jim also has a natural leadership skill that makes people want to follow him.

His leadership acumen causes people to want to invest not just money in him and his company, but to also invest themselves in the company to make it better. You really see this when you witness him interact with the individual managers, district managers, operations team, and anyone else on the Pilot Company team. There is such an evident sense of respect and admiration that every team member has for him.

At the board meetings, Big Jim can definitely lighten the atmosphere, but he can also start a meeting on time and end a meeting on time. He does not mess around when it comes to getting the business of the company done with efficiency and excellence. You cannot create a company of the size and with the success of Pilot Company without having an uncanny ability to galvanize various points of view and various interests into cohesive action among the teammates. Big Jim certainly has been able to do this, which is no doubt reflected all the way back to his sports career when he developed this affinity for teamwork. And yet, within this teamwork, he has always been acknowledged for his outstanding *individual* performance.

However, nothing has taught me as much about Big Jim as his reaction during a difficult time when the company was accused of misbehavior in its dealings with customers. Ultimately, he admitted that the company needed to make changes, but the most interesting thing to me was Big Jim's genuine attitude of sadness during this time. He had worked so hard to create a company deeply rooted in doing the right thing and treating people with respect. The accusation obviously affected him, but having to acknowledge that people in his company had behaved in a way that was so different from what he stood for was very difficult for him. This revealed so much about his character and his expectations regarding the character of the whole company. I think this says a lot about him as a human being. His mode was never to cover up or protect. Instead, he focused on the fact that the company had to be better than this because this was not what they stood for.

My first impressions in the White House were accurate. Big Jim is a really good guy with a positive outlook and a great sense of humor, but he is also a man of deep character and leadership. In other words, one should never underestimate his skills just because he can add a smile to the discussion. You cannot create a company of this breadth and scope without possessing the ability to be serious when you need to be serious … and Jim Haslam is serious about the right things.